Two Kings And Three Prophets For Less Than A Quarter

*First Lesson Sermons For
Sundays After Pentecost (First Third)
Cycle C*

Robert Leslie Holmes

CSS Publishing Company, Inc., Lima, Ohio

TWO KINGS AND THREE PROPHETS FOR LESS THAN A QUARTER

Copyright © 2000 by
CSS Publishing Company, Inc.
Lima, Ohio

All rights reserved. No part of this publication may be reproduced in any manner whatsoever without the prior permission of the publisher, except in the case of brief quotations embodied in critical articles and reviews. Inquiries should be addressed to: Permissions, CSS Publishing Company, Inc., P.O. Box 4503, Lima, Ohio 45802-4503.

Some scripture quotations are from the *New Revised Standard Version of the Bible*, copyright 1989 by the Division of Christian Education of the National Council of the Churches of Christ in the USA. Used by permission.

Library of Congress Cataloging-in-Publication Data

Holmes, Robert Leslie, 1945-
   Two kings and three prophets for less than a quarter : first lesson sermons for Sundays after Pentecost (first third) : Cycle C / Robert Leslie Holmes.
     p. cm.
   ISBN 0-7880-1719-5 (alk. paper)
   1. Pentecost season—Sermons. I. Title: 2 kings and 3 prophets for less than a quarter. II. Title.
BV4300.5 .H65 2000
252'.64—dc21   00-035805
                                                                                                      CIP

This book is available in the following formats, listed by ISBN:
   0-7880-1719-5   Book
   0-7880-1720-9   Disk
   0-7880-1721-7   Sermon Prep

For more information about CSS Publishing Company resources, visit our website at www.csspub.com.

PRINTED IN U.S.A.

For Barbara
To Disoscourus, a strong-willed daughter;
To Middle Age believers, a Holy Helper;
To me, a daily reminder that
God loves me very much.

Table Of Contents

Introduction	7
Pentecost Laughing In The Face Of Darkness! Acts 2:1-21	11
Holy Trinity Once Before A Time! Proverbs 8:1-4, 22-31	17
Corpus Christi The Sacrament Of War And Peace! Genesis 14:18-20	23
Proper 4 **Pentecost 2** **Ordinary Time 9** Make Up Your Mind! 1 Kings 18:20-39	29
Proper 5 **Pentecost 3** **Ordinary Time 10** Secondhand Religion 1 Kings 17:8-24	35
Proper 6 **Pentecost 4** **Ordinary Time 11** Bad News From A Good Man! 1 Kings 21:1-21a	41

Proper 7 47
Pentecost 5
Ordinary Time 12
    The Second Touch For The Out Of Touch!
    1 Kings 19:1-15a

Proper 8 55
Pentecost 6
Ordinary Time 13
    One Fired-Up Preacher!
    2 Kings 2:1-2, 6-14

Proper 9 61
Pentecost 7
Ordinary Time 14
    The ABC Gospel
    2 Kings 5:1-14

Proper 10 67
Pentecost 8
Ordinary Time 15
    Plumb Line Prophecy
    Amos 7:7-17

Lectionary Preaching After Pentecost 75

Introduction

"An obligation is laid on me, and woe to me if I do not proclaim the gospel!" (1 Corinthians 9:16). If you are reading this book there is a good chance that you have felt the obligation to preach, for this is, first and foremost, a book for preachers. Moreover, it is a book written by a preacher. You and I are, together, the custodians of the most important information this world will ever hear. Every day millions of people all across the world tune in for the nightly news on television. The reality is that the nightly news delivered by those people we watch (bless them all) was most likely written by someone else and not the newsreader. What is more, the news will be different tomorrow. There is nothing constant about it. It might be said that its only certainty is that it changes every day. The news committed to our safekeeping is different in that those who preach it usually compose it themselves and it never changes. For two millennia now the message has been the same. That, in itself, presents an extra challenge that few people, who do not preach, can understand. It is only the package in which we deliver it that changes.

This is our message: God loves the world and gave his Son, Jesus, to save it. How many different ways are there to say that? That, in a sense, was a challenge that intrigued the brilliant Winston Churchill to the point of perplexity when, after he was voted out of office, someone suggested that he put his significant oratorical skills to use as a preacher. "Anyone who thinks he can deliver the same message to the same crowd week after week whilst continuing to hold their attention is a fool," said he. He continued, "I may have lost an election, but I am not a fool!" What Sir Winston failed to understand is that it is possible to deliver the same message week upon week and hold the people's attention. For when we preach, another stands beside us and empowers our message. It is the One who loved us all the way to Calvary and loves us still. In his name, God has entrusted us with a message that supercedes every other message in the world. In his name, God gives us the Holy Spirit who makes the message we preach new for every generation. In addition, God has given us a book so filled with truths around which to preach that we could never run out of things to say. And, so we preach!

This little volume has been fun to author largely because I love preaching and preachers. I send it forth with the prayer that God will use it to kindle your fire for the pulpit. As you might imagine, no one can write a book like this unaided. The seeds that spring forth here as stories have come to me from a variety of sources. While I have tried to give just credit where it is due, it is possible I have omitted credit someone believes is his or hers. Be assured that the omission is unintentional and please accept my apology.

Perhaps you are wondering about its title. As I wrote it, it dawned on me that the Lectionary assignments for this season come principally from the books of First and Second Kings and that the readings assigned focus principally on the ministries of three prophets, namely Elijah, Elisha, and Amos. Since the period assigned is just ten weeks and not a full quarter, I decided it might add to your joy in studying these passages if you could think of them as *Two Kings And Three Prophets For Less Than A Quarter.* There are, of course, others here, too. Some are true and some are false. They range from Abram to Melchizedek to Amaziah. Through their messages and their lifestyles, all have something to teach us whether good or not good. Yet, in this short season it is in the books of the Kings with Elijah and Elisha and in Amos that we find our primary gateway to talking about the King of kings, the Lord who loves us. So, even as I have had fun in preparing this manuscript for publication, may you also have fun as you read it and take its message to heart.

The words on these pages are in a lot better shape because my wife Barbara has reviewed them. For her encouragement and assistance with this project, I am very grateful. The people of Pittsburgh's First Presbyterian Church have been generous in their encouragement for me to write and have made it possible for me to do so. I am thankful to them as well. Especially to be mentioned are the members of our church staff and, in particular, Betty Chapman, my assistant. Without their encouragement, and especially without Betty, I would never find the time to write. Debra Meyer of our "First Church Family" provided invaluable assistance in reading the galley proofs. Her skills and suggestions have improved the finished product immeasurably. Thank you, Debra. Also deserving of special mention is Tom Lentz of CSS Publishing who first approached me about doing this project. I appreciate the trust he placed in me and hope he now feels it was not such a bad idea after all. Finally, I am grateful to you, the reader. Without you there would be no need to do this book or any of the others I have written or edited. I pray that you will find in these pages not only ideas for sermons but food to nourish your soul. As you read these words, stop occasionally to remember that you are being prayed for, because you are. May God enrich your life and ministry through what is said here. And, may I ask one favor as I close? That is, would you please pray for me when you say your prayers?

Finally, a word for those who read this book with a goal other than preaching: it comes to you with my special prayer that God will use its message to strengthen your life and enrich your walk with him. May you find here food that nourishes your soul in Christ's service.

Soli Deo Gloria!

Robert Leslie Holmes
Pittsburgh, Pennsylvania
(Philippians 1:9-11)

Pentecost

Laughing In The Face Of Darkness!

Acts 2:1-21

A seminary student writing a term paper about confession of sin started to type, "When we confess, Christ takes away our guilt." However, he was a bit thick-fingered and hit the letter q instead of the letter g on his computer keyboard. Now his sentence read, "Christ takes away our quilt." He didn't notice his error but his professor did and wrote in the margin, "Fear not, little one, you'll not freeze for God has given us a Comforter!" Using his keen wit, the professor conveyed a profound spiritual truth that is at the heart of Pentecost. God has given us a Comforter. However, it is also true to say that when the Comforter comes, God takes away our quilt. That is, God removes our security blankets that we sometimes wrap around ourselves and that cause us to miss the exciting life that is available for all of us who belong to Jesus. That finally is what Pentecost Sunday is about. So, today we think about the personal meaning of Pentecost.

Wouldn't you like to know that God has all of you there is to have and that you have all of God you can have? Surely you would agree that anything less than that is second class spirituality. God's presence was made known to the 120 people in the Upper Room in a dramatically sensational way. The Bible says there was a violent wind. In addition to the wind, there was fire and the Holy Spirit came. What can we expect when the Holy Spirit comes to us, when Pentecost is personal?

The proofs of a personal Pentecost are essentially two, according to Acts 2:4. There is a definite experience that is accompanied by real evidence. Listen: "All of them were filled with the Holy

Spirit [the experience of Pentecost] and began [there is the evidence of Pentecost] to speak in other languages, as the Spirit gave them ability." Before that, their hearts were heavy. At the Last Supper they had made their commitments to Jesus known. Then came the betrayal by Judas, the denial by Peter, and the desertion by the others. They had seen or heard about Jesus dying on the cross. They had witnessed the appearance of the risen Lord, the death defeater. Following that, Christ was taken from them again, and again they were in a holding pattern. The future looked uncertain, perhaps even bleak. It held no guarantees, for the future never does. They wanted something wonderful to happen and it did. In the face of their darkness, they found new joy and laughed again. It happened at Pentecost. That is what makes Pentecost Sunday such an important day in the life of the church around the world. Today, however, I want to come down from that and take the spotlight of the world and narrow the beam a bit. I want you to sense with me something of the personal meaning of Pentecost; something that will clear away our doubts, remove our fears; something that will lift you above the drone of the nightly news and make faith come alive. I want us together to laugh in the face of the darkness and doubt that surrounds us in this world we live in. Wouldn't you like to know a relationship with Jesus that would lift you above the doldrums of day-to-day life and make faith alive? I know that is what I want. Don't you?

First, a word of caution seems to be in order. Scripture warns us, "Do not be conformed to this world, but be transformed by the renewing of your minds" (Romans 12:2). Another way to translate the beginning of that verse is, "Don't let the world around you shape you by its mold." In the same way, we should be careful that we do not try to cast God the Holy Spirit into a mold of our own making. In 1 Kings 19:10-13, Elijah felt he needed to hear God's voice in a new way. There was a mighty wind, an earthquake and, finally, a fire. It sounds like an early version of Pentecost, doesn't it? Yet, it was not. The Bible says that when God came, it was in the form of a still small voice, a whisper so gentle that it was barely audible. Sometimes God uses dramatic means of bringing Pentecost home to us and sometimes God speaks through gentle whispers. Sometimes he gets our attention through a tornado and sometimes it is through the gentle whimper of a tiny baby. The point is: do not fall for the temptation of measuring someone else's experience of Pentecost by your own, nor your own by someone else's. Don't try to make God meet your standards, for you will often be disappointed and always wrong when you do that. Allow God to be the Lord of Pentecost for you and others, and know that Pentecost comes sometimes through mighty winds and fire and sometimes through gentle whispers. The important point is that it comes, for Pentecost must come if we belong to Jesus. It came for the disciples in experience and with evidence.

I. The Pentecost Experience

"All of them were filled with the Holy Spirit." That is a historical record of what truly happened one day in Jerusalem. The disciples were waiting in the Upper Room when suddenly God's Spirit came upon them. It was real. Life for them would never be the same again.

It is a real and life-transforming experience for us too. The experience of Pentecost, the coming of the Holy Spirit, is as real for Christians today as it was 2,000 years ago in Jerusalem. In fact, God commands us to experience it. "Be filled with the Spirit" (Ephesians 5:18). The Greek is a commanding imperative. This personal Pentecost is meant to be part of a normal Christian experience. "They were all filled." Did you catch that, "*All*"? How many were filled with the Holy Spirit? Not a few of them; not many of them; not even most of them. All of them were! Later Peter would preach to them, "Repent, and be baptized every one of you...." All! Every one of you! Are you getting the universality of the Pentecost experience for Christians?

To experience Pentecost is to undergo the normal fruit of salvation. It is not a second step in salvation that creates two classes of Christians. It is a normal part of every Christian's life. Last December a friend of mine was experiencing difficulties with his watch. Sometimes that watch would run just fine. For days it kept perfect time. Then, suddenly and with no warning, it stopped. It was quite unreliable. He attempted to have it repaired with no success. Well, Christmas was coming and he decided to drop a few hints around his family about needing a new watch but no one seemed to pick up on them. So, he started looking around the stores, planning to buy one for himself. He saw some watches he liked, but he could not decide which one he liked best. Christmas morning came and his children wakened him. He wondered how they were up at such an early hour, for his watch said it was just after two o'clock. When he protested, his wife pointed out that according to all the other clocks in their home it was almost seven o'clock. His watch was stopped again. The family went downstairs and there, beneath the tree, was a new watch that had been placed in a disguised box and carefully wrapped sometime before. What he needed he possessed all along without realizing it. When it comes to the Holy Spirit the same principle holds true for some Christians. What they need to do is not receive the Holy Spirit but to stir up the Spirit that is already within them.

"Rekindle the gift of God that is within you," Paul told his young son in the ministry (2 Timothy 1:6). Clearly Timothy already had the gift of the Spirit but, in the face of opposition from some people in his community, Timothy had wilted like a leaf in a drought. He was all caught up in the darkness of his present circumstances. Perhaps today you need to rekindle God's Spirit in your life. Long ago you made your profession of faith in Jesus and, for a while now, you have lapsed. Your faith, which once blazed like fire, has died away and there is barely a glowing ember in the hearth of your heart. All around you, you feel encompassed by the darkness. Today, on this Pentecost Sunday, I say to you in the name of Jesus Christ, "Come alive again in the Spirit. Be renewed and restored to your first love for Christ. Remove your quilt. Be done with your sin and your doubt. Give up your security blanket. Let nothing hold you back from being the person you were meant to be in the Lord!" When you do you will not only experience Pentecost again, your life shall once again bear the evidence of Pentecost.

II. The Pentecost Evidence

"All of them were filled with the Holy Spirit and began...." Our personal Pentecost always has a beginning place. There is invariably a decisive moment. *"They began,"* was the moment of decision for the disciples in the Upper Room. Anything of consequence in our lives has some beginning point. There was a day or a moment when you decided to say, "Yes." "Yes, I will go back to school." "Yes, I will study to become something more than I am." "Yes, I will ask her to marry me." "Yes, I will accept his proposal." "They began." Let this be your beginning point to a new level of commitment to Christ in the power of his Holy Spirit.

"All of them were filled with the Holy Spirit and began to speak in other languages, as the Spirit gave them ability." Speaking in tongues was the evidence that Pentecost had come home for them. For you, as for most Christians, the evidence may be different. The essential evidence of Pentecost was not that they spoke in tongues but that they began, at that moment, to be vital and effective in their work for the Lord. You see, Pentecost really begins not when we speak but when we listen and obey. Elijah had to listen for the whisper of the still small voice, and we must listen for God's voice to come to us. When we listen, he will speak. When he speaks we must obey.

"They began" to be powerful and effective witnesses: "You will receive power when the Holy Spirit has come upon you; and you will be my witnesses in Jerusalem, in all Judea and Samaria, and to the ends of the earth" (Acts 1:8). "With great power the apostles gave their testimony to the resurrection of the Lord Jesus" (Acts 4:33). "Those who were scattered went from place to place, proclaiming the word" (Acts 8:4). Part of the evidence that we belong to Christ, and that Pentecost has come to us, is that we can no longer remain quiet about Jesus. We can no more be quiet than the sea can cease being wet or the birds can stop singing. Through Joel the prophet, God said, "I will pour out my spirit on all flesh; your sons and your daughters shall prophesy" (Joel 2:28). Are you telling the story of Jesus? If you've begun your personal Pentecost, you are. "For we cannot keep from speaking about what we have seen and heard" (Acts 4:20).

"They began" to be willing to suffer the consequences of building up Christ's kingdom. In Acts 5 we read that after the disciples had been before the Sanhedrin some counsel members wanted to

kill them. How did they respond? "As they left the council, they rejoiced that they were considered worthy to suffer dishonor for the sake of the name. And every day in the temple and at home they did not cease to teach and proclaim Jesus as the Messiah" (Acts 5:41-42). They laughed in the face of suffering. Jesus said that following him would mean taking up a cross every day. Have you worn your cross today? Did you wear it yesterday? For Christ the gospel meant a rough Roman cross. For the disciples also, it meant death. Why should we imagine that it will mean no suffering for us? Are you ready, Church, to bear your burden, carry your cross, do your duty, no matter how unpleasant, for Jesus Christ? That, too, is part of Pentecost.

"*They began*" to live new life in the Spirit because they knew that God had brought into their lives an experience of meaning and purpose the like of which they had not known before. The same God, through the same Jesus, comes today on Pentecost in the power of the same Spirit to do great things in and through you. He will raise you up to life on a higher plane. He will set your feet on a rock that cannot be moved, fill you with his joy, and cause you to laugh in the face of any darkness this world can bring. When will you say yes to him? When will you welcome the Holy Spirit for your personal Pentecost? Why not now? Wouldn't it be wonderful if your new life in the Spirit began today?

Holy Trinity

Once Before A Time!

Proverbs 8:1-4, 22-31

During a serious shortage of currency in Great Britain, thousands of people were starving and many were naked and homeless because there was no money with which they could be paid or buy life's necessities. Oliver Cromwell selected a group of men to scour the land for silver that might be used to give those people what they needed so that they could be properly housed, fed, and clothed. For months they traversed the British Empire and returned to bring this report: "We have searched the empire and found very little silver save that which is in the great cathedrals where images of saints are constructed of the finest silver." Cromwell was initially discouraged but a few days later he hit upon an idea. Calling his men together, he issued this order: "Let's melt down those saints and put them into circulation to help the less fortunate."

On this Trinity Sunday I want to suggest to you that God has committed to you and me the wisdom of the ages and that we have a Christ-given responsibility to melt down and put ourselves in circulation among the needy so we might bring them to Jesus.

We've all heard those stories that begin, "Once upon a time." Today's Scripture reading from Proverbs begins, "Once before time." It refers to eternity past where God alone existed and made some great plans. Our Bible reading begins and ends with a call to attention and confronts us with the fact that every human being has a natural capacity for folly against which we struggle to find God's wisdom. Wisdom is what the Book of Proverbs is finally all about. The first nine chapters contrast wisdom and folly. Solomon is writing to his son who is about to graduate into adulthood. He approaches his subject with the concern that any caring parent has at that point. He wants his son to know that wisdom and folly each are bidding for his life. Folly is to follow one's own path and plan for life, and that is our natural inclination. Wisdom is to get in touch with the Triune God and to invest one's life in what God is about in the world. Our natural inclination must be brought into submission if we are to be and do what God made us for. We are, if you will, like those fine-silver cathedral saints. We can follow folly and look good but we will not accomplish much. To follow wisdom, on the other hand, is to spend our lives involved in a cause that is of infinite value to God. Solomon, author of these Proverbs, writes, "To you, O people, I call, and my cry is to all that live." Real wisdom is to recognize from whence we came and to consider where our pathway leads us.

I. Once Before A Time God Was The Source Of Our Being

"The Lord created me at the beginning of his work, the first of his acts of long ago" (Proverbs 8:22).

The Hebrew word translated *"created me"* actually means "to be possessed or known intimately." It means that not only did God plan our lives before all time, but that he still has an interest in us and a wonderful plan for our lives. From the beginning God has owned us and known all about us. Compare Solomon's words to what Saint Paul tells the Ephesians, "He chose us in Christ before the foundation of the world to be holy and blameless before him in love" (Ephesians 1:4). Once before a time, God planned our coming. None of us is here by accident. Each of us was created in the mind of God before time began and we were created with a mission in mind. That mission, according to one old catechism, is "to glorify God, and enjoy him forever."[1] Until we recognize that, and respond to it appropriately, all our life, no matter how smart it appears on the outside, is spent chasing rainbows. It is folly.

Isn't it amazing to think that when the Triune God made the world, you were already part of the plan! Further evidence of that is found in the verses following verse 22. Wise people know and respond to these facts: "I was set up, at the first, before the beginning of the earth. When there were no depths I was brought forth, when there were no springs abounding with water. Before the mountains had been shaped, before the hills, I was brought forth. When he had not yet made earth and fields, or the world's first bits of soil. When he established the heavens, I was there, when he drew a circle on the face of the deep" (8:23-27). When God did all these things, you were already a part of a plan. God the creator had us in mind for a mission before the beginning of the earth, before the sea or the mountains and hills or fields. It was his plan before the world began that we would be doing his work in it, as saints in circulation. Now you begin to understand, do you not, why when sin interrupted God's plan he thought so much of you that "He gave his only Son, so that everyone who believes in him may not perish but may have eternal life" (John 3:16).

In one of his hymns, Isaac Watts puts it this way:

> *Well might the sun in darkness hide,*
> *And shut his glories in,*
> *When Christ the Mighty Maker died,*
> *For man the creature's sin.*[2]

II. Once Before A Time God Saw All Things

David says it well, "Great is our Lord, and abundant in power; his understanding is beyond measure" (Psalm 147:5). But, it is even better than that. God saw all that would be before the world was made. For God there are no surprises. He sees our future and our past with equal clarity. "I know the plans I have for you, says the Lord, plans for your welfare and not for harm, to give you a future with hope" (Jeremiah 29:11).

We're not like that. Our minds are limited. Our best plans have short horizons. But God's understanding, like his grace, has no boundaries. We try to understand. Some of us try in all kinds of ways to get a grasp on the future, from teacups and palm readings to horoscopes and tarot cards. In truth, however, even the past is too complicated for us to understand. Americans spend millions of dollars each year with psychoanalysts trying to understand how all the pieces of the past fit together. God already knows for "his understanding is beyond measure." If we put our hand in his, our past with all its sin and murky history is taken care of and our tomorrow will always be better than it could ever be without him. He already knows what is ahead.

Some years ago there was a popular comic strip called *Mutt and Jeff*. Perhaps you remember it. In one strip Mutt found Jeff sitting on a sidewalk curbside weeping sorely. "Why are you crying?" Mutt asked him. "I'm crying because my little boy just got run over by a pickup truck," Jeff replied. "But, you don't have a little boy!" Mutt protested. "I know," responded Jeff, "but as I sat here watching the traffic I began to think about how nice it would be to own one of these fancy cars. Then I thought, 'What if I was to invite the prettiest girl in town to go out driving with me and she accepted, and what if we fell in love and got married, and what if we had a wonderful little boy!' Gosh, wouldn't that be wonderful?" "So," asked Mutt, "why does that idea make you cry?" "Well," Jeff replied, "it wasn't that idea that made me cry. It was when I thought, 'What if our little boy ran out on the road one day and a pickup truck couldn't stop and ran over him?' " He started to boo-hoo all over again.

It sounds silly, does it not? Yet, some of us go through life wondering, "What if?" "What if I fail my next test in school?" "What if the market crashes?" "What if I lose my job?" "What if my marriage fails?" "What if my roof starts to leak?" In his later years, Mark Twain said, "I've known a great many troubles in my life, but most of them never happened." That is how it is with our "what ifs" too.

Some of our "what ifs" are not about what might happen but about what did happen: "What if I'd done something differently?" "What if I'd never done that?" Fulton Oursler said that many of us crucify ourselves between two thieves: regret for yesterday and fear for tomorrow. He was right! When we have a "what if" attitude to life, we will always end up crying somewhere — if not on the curb of a sidewalk then somewhere else. That "what if" mentality comes from not trusting the all-seeing wisdom of a loving God to guide and guard our lives and obeying his commandments.

Are we talking about predestination, that doctrine that turns many Christians cold? No. We are talking about an eternally existent triune

God, who reveals himself as Father, Son, and Holy Spirit, whose plan for all time is well thought out. His plan took into account that people would love darkness rather than light (see John 3:19). He designed a manger in Bethlehem where the Son of God would lie as a baby and a cross where God's Son would hang at Calvary and pay the penalty our sin demands. That plan was designed because God the Father loved us and sought to bring us a new opportunity for righteousness through Jesus Christ. The message of Christ's love is brought to us today in the power of God the Holy Spirit. That is the kind of God you need and not some willy-nilly wimp of a deity whose plan was an exercise in disarrangement.

III. Once Before A Time God Enacted A Wonderful Plan For The Universe

"We speak God's wisdom, secret and hidden, which God decreed before the ages for our glory" (1 Corinthians 2:7).

Do you remember the old "Tin Lizzie," the Model T Ford? In his book, *Hearts of Iron, Feet of Clay*,[3] Gary Inrig tells about a young fellow whose Model T was off on the side of a road with its hood up. He was trying desperately to repair it but having no success. At the point of frustration and ready to quit, he watched as a sleek, chauffeur-driven limousine pulled off the road behind him. Out stepped a well-dressed man who watched the young man fiddle with the engine for a while. In a moment the newcomer suggested that the young man make a minor adjustment to one part. The young man, skeptical about strangers, did what was suggested only because nothing else he had tried worked. "Now," said the stranger, "crank it up." So, the young fellow took hold of the crank on the front of the car and turned it one time. Suddenly the motor burst to life and began to purr better than ever before. Amazed that such a well-dressed fellow knew so much about cars, the young man asked him, "How did you know what to do?" "Well," replied the stranger, "I'm Henry Ford and I made this car, so I know all about how it works."

God who made this world knows all about it and all about us. When you get frustrated because it doesn't go your way, remember him. He knows how to fix things!

The eternal triune God alone is all-wise over events in the past, present, and future. It is not mere chance that causes events to come together in our lives. It is a sovereign God who works in all things for our good. No wonder, then, that Paul exclaims, "O the depth of the riches and wisdom and knowledge of God! How unsearchable are his judgments and how inscrutable his ways! For who has known the mind of the Lord? Or who has been his counselor?" (Romans 11:33-34).

This is the One who comes to you now and calls you to action in his kingdom. Put yourself in circulation for his glory and you will never regret it. May it be today that we would hear his eternally wise voice deep within our souls and with once-doubting Thomas come alive for Christ's sake, confessing, "My Lord and my God!" That would be wise. In the name of the Father and of the Son and of the Holy Spirit. Amen.

---

1. *Westminster Shorter Catechism*, written by the Westminster Assembly in 1647 as a concise question and answer instructional tool for use by Christians.

2. From the hymn, *Alas! And Did My Savior Bleed,* Isaac Watts (1707).

3. Inrig, Gary. *Hearts of Iron, Feet of Clay,* (Chicago: Moody Press, 1979), pp. 111-112.

Corpus Christi

The Sacrament Of War And Peace!

Genesis 14:18-20

As dawn awakened one August morning over a tiny French village called Pielo, its citizens were herded into the village square to face a Nazi firing squad. It was 1944 and the enemy had routed out a small unit of French underground freedom fighters in the village the night before. Among the villagers was a fifteen-year-old boy. He did not really understand why, but he knew that the intention of the occupying forces was to shoot them all. He looked at the villagers all around him and realized that almost all of them were older than he was. They had lived a long time. He thought about how much life he was going to miss. More than anything else, the thought of being shot to death scared him. He wondered what might happen if he were shot and terribly wounded but did not die right away. Would he be able to bear the pain? What would the bullets feel like as they barreled through his body? All these and many other thoughts rushed through his mind. Suddenly a sound like an explosion somewhere in the distance caught his attention. It was followed by the noise of tanks approaching his village. Were more Nazis coming to hasten the slaughter? Or, could he be dreaming and this was a friendly force coming to their rescue? There had been rumors, coming mostly from the resistance, that help was on the way and perhaps freedom. A German officer barked out a command to his troops. In an instant the Nazi soldiers scattered to take cover in nearby buildings against a unit of American GIs that was at that moment rounding the corner and entering the village square. It was true! His greatest dream was coming true! He and his neighbors from the village were being rescued from the jaws of death.

Corporal Bob Hamsley led the Americans. He shouted for the villagers to run and take cover. They did. For three hours there was shooting until finally fifty Nazis lay dead and another fifty were taken prisoner. Nearly half a century later the people of Pielo remembered that day in a special ceremony in the Village Square. The guest of honor at that ceremony was a man who had traveled back to Pielo from the United States. His name was Bob Hamsley, and the mayor of what was now the town of Pielo had invited him to receive the city key. Although they had met only briefly for one moment in time, that fifteen-year-old boy, now a grown man and mayor of his town, would never forget the day he almost died in a hail of Nazi bullets, nor the man who saved his life and brought peace to his village. As mayor, he had gone to great lengths to find him and invite him to this celebration of remembrance and freedom.

I tell this story because today's text from Genesis 14 was also born out of war and peace. A raiding enemy took prisoner Abram's nephew Lot. When Abram learned what had happened, he immediately rose up and tried to rescue him. War is always an ugly thing, but sometimes war is a necessary thing. There are times when circumstances beyond our control force us to get involved in situations we would rather avoid. Abram, despite his small number of soldiers and their lack of experience, was victorious and "King Melchizedek of Salem brought out bread and wine; he was priest of God Most High" (Genesis 14:18). So, you see that this sacrament was also born in war and, strangely enough, peace as well.

I. This Sacrament Was Born In War

It is true that King Melchizedek greeted Abram. Melchizedek means "King of righteousness." He was a man whose heart was tuned to God, and his character and his reputation reflected it. He was king of Salem, a word that is from the same root as *shalom*, meaning peace. Shalom is more than freedom from the disturbance of outside conflicts. It is peace within the soul. Salem, the region Melchizedek ruled, would eventually be called Jerusalem. Jerusalem means the City of Peace.

Melchizedek was at the same time a king and a priest and he was good at both jobs. In fact, he was so good that the highest honor that could be given to any priest after him was to be called "a priest forever according to the order of Melchizedek" (Psalm 110:4). A priest is an agent of righteousness and peace. The lesson that comes out of Melchizedek's life is, "Live for God and he will use you and raise you up."

There is another reason why I can say that this sacrament was born out of war. Another kingly priest, our Prince of Peace, Jesus Christ, instituted it. Jesus "took a loaf of bread, and after blessing it he broke it, gave it to them, and said, 'Take; this is my body.' Then he took a cup, and after giving thanks he gave it to them, and all of them drank from it. He said to them, 'This is my blood of the covenant, which is poured out for many. Truly I tell you, I will never again drink of the fruit of the vine until that day when I drink it new in the kingdom of God'" (Matthew 14:22-25). A war raged between heaven and hell, good and evil, righteousness and unrighteousness, God and Satan. Our Lord Jesus Christ came to bring it to a conclusion. He gives us his assurance that sufficient sacrifice has been made on his cross to atone for all our sins and bring us peace like none the world can ever offer. So in this sacrament we celebrate war. Yet, we also celebrate victory and peace.

II. This Sacrament Is Bathed In Victory

"Thanks be to God, who gives us the victory through our Lord Jesus Christ" (1 Corinthians 15:57). The victory is all ours because in his death on the cross, which we recall through this sacrament, we learn that the penalty for our sins was paid in full and that our peace with God has been made possible. Christ's death was followed by his resurrection. The resurrection of Jesus brings us victory over death and the grave. It promises us victory over sin for the Scriptures say, "If we confess our sins, he who is faithful and just will forgive us our sins and cleanse us from all unrighteousness" (1 John 1:9).

> *The strife is o'er, the battle done;*
> *The victory of life is won;*
> *Our song of triumph has begun.*
> *Alleluia!*
>
> *The powers of death had done their worst;*
> *But Christ their legions hath dispersed;*
> *Let shouts of holy joy outburst.*
> *Alleluia!*
>
> *Lord, by the stripes that wounded Thee;*
> *From death's dread sting thy servants free;*
> *That we may live and sing to Thee.*
> *Alleluia!*[1]

Do you know this victory? Have you given your life unto Almighty Christ our Priest and King? Have you given him your sins and claimed the forgiveness that is found only in him? If so, let us celebrate the victory as we participate together in the Sacrament in his name.

III. This Sacrament Brings Us Peace

"King Melchizedek of Salem brought out bread and wine." Salem, as I said, comes from the same Hebrew root as shalom, the ancient Hebrew word for peace. Despite its tragic history, Jerusalem is, in fact, the City of Peace. Thus, Melchizedek's title is truly "King of the peace place." Although he and Abram were strangers to each other, and although they were together only for this day and this meal, they became instant friends. Their peace was symbolized through the bread and wine in a moment Abram would never forget.

Jesus, the Lord at this table, is our King of Peace. He says, "My peace I give to you. I do not give to you as the world gives. Do not let your hearts be troubled, and do not let them be afraid" (John 14:27). In this Sacrament, Jesus Christ comes anew to offer you his peace through his blood shed on the cross.

Peace! Peace of mind and heart are still are our most precious and needed experiences. In his book, *A Time to Heal,* President

Gerald Ford repeats a story he heard some years before when he was a young Congressman. During the 1948 civil war in Greece, a villager was planning to emigrate to the United States. Before he left he asked his weary, beleaguered, poverty-stricken neighbors what they would like him to send home once he arrived in America. "Would you like money? Food? Clothes?" "No," responded one of his neighbors, "you should send us a ton of tranquility."

A ton of peace! How much is that? I suspect what his neighbor wanted was the yoke of national war to be lifted off him and his friends in order that the people of Greece might find peace again. I would also suggest that there is a greater peace than the absence of conflict, however. It is the shalom peace that encompasses not only our outward circumstances but also our inner being. Wouldn't you like to know a peace like that? It is found in your Prince of Peace, Jesus. You can receive it now by faith as you participate at this table. "Since we are justified by faith, we have peace with God through our Lord Jesus Christ" (Romans 5:1). If you have never done it before, I invite you in Christ's name to make your peace with God today. It will be a day you will never forget.

---

1. Latin hymn translated by Francis Pott (1861).

Proper 4 • Pentecost 2 • Ordinary Time 9

Make Up Your Mind!

1 Kings 18:20-39

Why hasn't Hollywood made this into a major motion picture epic? 1 Kings 18 is surely one of the most dramatic accounts in all literature and one of the most significant historical records in the Bible. Its message and natural application are timeless.

William Penn said, "Men must be governed by God or they will be ruled by tyrants." In our Scripture reading for today the people of Israel came together to decide no less a question than who would govern their personal and national lives, who would be their God and the God of their nation.

I. What Kind Of God Do You Believe In?
"What kind of God do you believe in?" It was not that the people of Israel had no god. They were, in truth, very spiritual. They had many gods, called Baals. The Baals were alluring gods who could be worshiped according to the momentary dictates of the flesh and lustful imagination. They included Baals of power, sex, money, popularity, and prestige. No wonder they were popular! The Israelites also paid homage to the true God. After all, he was the One who had delivered their ancestors out of bondage. To give up on him completely would be a mark of disrespect to their forebears. They could never fully give up on the God of their national heritage, and so they politely included him with quick nod-of-the-head acknowledgments as they went about their own business. As a result, the religion of the true God and the Baals became entangled in their national mindset through the process of time. They failed to remember that "I the Lord your God am a jealous

God, punishing children for the iniquity of parents, to the third and the fourth generation" (Exodus 20:5). Elijah confronted them with this truth in the name of Jehovah and forced them to answer the question of national and personal loyalty. It could not be God and the Baals. It had to be God *or* the Baals.

A fellow attending a major league baseball game caused a bit of a stir in the stands. No matter which team made a hit or a run, he cheered. Finally, curiosity caught someone behind him. Leaning forward, the second man asked, "Why are you rooting for both teams? Don't you understand this game?" By way of response the first one replied, "I live too far away to get to a ballgame like this more than once every couple of years, so I pull for both teams. That way, no matter who wins, I go home happy." You don't have to be a sports fan to know that if you have any sense of loyalty to the home team, you will not root for both sides. "No one can serve two masters" (Matthew 6:24) is a principle that has application for sports as well as for religion.

Yet, that is exactly what we seem to be attempting in our current quest for pluralism pushed to extremes. Today America has moved from the "one nation under God" commitment described in our Pledge of Allegiance to a nation of multi-faceted deities who present themselves in a plethora of variations on a theme. We are not, as is sometimes said of us, a godless nation. We are, rather, a nation of many gods. You can hear the hymns and confessions of our pluralistic deities, often sung at the same time, in all the trendy places from university campuses to the media and even in the church sometimes. We have no fixed standards. We have lived through a subtle theological gearshift from believing in God to believing in spirituality. No longer is the God of the Bible central to our understanding of deity and worship. Instead, we have become devotees of a faith that sets personal experience above God's truth revealed in the Bible. Doctrine and dogma have given way to something called "cosmic consciousness" or the "true self." America being what it is, a place where consumerism and popular opinion polls determine what matters, it should not surprise us to know that millions of dollars are spent to promote this trendy phenomenon. At this dawning of the new millennium, religion and spirituality have gotten all mixed up like the ingredients in a cement mixer, except nothing solid or lasting will come of this hybrid thing we call religion.

I believe that America today faces the same choice that Israel did when Elijah called the people to meet on Mount Carmel. There is perhaps no more telling evidence of it than the response of many to the ugly crisis in the White House and Congress just two years or so ago. Attempts to replace the Constitution with the latest popular opinion polls were telling evidence of how our nation is spiritually adrift. We saw that many of our leaders have, in Stephen Vincent Benet's words, "no fixed stars." God's standards of morality and truth possess little relevance or authority for many people in our time and place. Sociologists and historians say that America has entered a post-Christian era, and it is fair to ask if we are even a Constitutional nation. More's the pity for, "Where there is no prophecy, the people cast off restraint" (Proverbs 29:18). When anything goes, one of the first things a nation loses is God's sure hand of mercy, guidance, and blessing.

In their book, *The Fourth Turning: An American Prophecy*,[1] historical sociologists William Strauss and Neil Howe have done some intriguing research with America's history, viewing events through the lens of each generation and making some projections about the future. To be short, their picture is not promising. They predict that within a few years there will be an American crisis on the scale of the American Revolution, the Civil War, or the Crash of '29. So how do we prepare for it, just in case they are right? Do we stockpile food, water, and guns, and store our money in jelly jars in the backyard? Or, do we ask ourselves what really matters? Who is my God? What rules and principles shall guide the way I live this life entrusted to me?

Whatever else we do, we should know where our commitment lies. It is my responsibility to tell you this! You have already decided. Whether or not Strauss and Howe are right in their estimation of our future, I cannot say. Of this, however, I can be sure: I have an obligation to my God to warn you that any life where he is not given his proper place, whether it is national or personal, is a life lived on the edge of destruction. "If the sentinel sees the sword coming and does not blow the trumpet, so that the people are not warned, and the sword comes and takes any of them, they are taken away in their iniquity, but their blood I will require at the sentinel's hand" (Ezekiel 33:6). "Now if you are unwilling to serve the Lord, choose this day whom you will serve ... but as for me and my household, we will serve the Lord" (Joshua 24:15).

I am also certain of this: There is no neutral ground. If you think you can delay making a choice, you have already chosen, whether you realize it or not. When we, as a nation, try to root for two teams in the spiritual realm, when we pass on no settled values of right and wrong, our children will do what the Baal followers did. They will try to create a cocktail of deities, a god-blend. In the process, they will become unwitting slaves to the passions of each moment, much like the dogs in the street. Instead of being a beacon of hope, light, and leadership to the world, America will drift off as Rome, Greece, and old Israel did before us.

British school children a generation or so ago were taught a phrase designed to heighten their national pride. That phrase was, "The sun never sets on the British Empire." Watching the lowering of the flag over Hong Kong a couple of years ago, a friend of mine, who grew up in Britain remembered East African Church and business leaders in Nairobi, to whom he had traveled to speak, jeering in response to that phrase. You see, they too once were taught that phrase. From their own experiences and those of other former colonies, they knew that the sun had long ago set on the British Empire. In fact, they were living proof that it had, for they were, that very year, commemorating the twenty-fifth anniversary of independence as a church and nation. Their gathering itself was evidence that a once-great empire had fallen, in the space of little more than one generation, to become a second-rate power. What happened to the British Empire can happen to America. It is, in fact, already happening. We do well to remember Ezekiel's words when he cried out, "Turn back, turn back from your evil ways; for why will you die, O [America]?" (cf. Ezekiel 33:11).

II. The God Who Is There

Elijah called Israel to recognize that the true God has plans and standards that do not change and that will not be compromised. Behind them all stands His never failing love. Let it be said very clearly that true love is not demonstrated by permissiveness. A loving parent does not permit a child to do anything the child wants. A loving parent sets standards for the child's own good. That child, in turn, passes them along to the next generation. God, in love, has set standards for us and for America. "By this we know that we love the children of God, when we love God and obey his commandments. For the love of God is this, that we obey his commandments" (1 John 5:2-3). God loves us enough to set safe limits on us. We should do no less for our leaders and fellow citizens. To do less is to sin against this God who sends fire from heaven.

Dietrich Bonhoeffer became a World War II Christian martyr for refusing to join other church "leaders" in turning a blind-eye to Nazi terrorism. He said, "Only those who obey truly believe and those who believe truly obey." He knew that belief and obedience go together like the two sides of a coin. One side is worthless without the other. The Bible's God is not a by-product of momentary passions or fanciful imaginations. He is the Creator of all things good and they were called into being by his mighty power. "Popular" opinion, no matter how popular, cannot change his nature and laws.

The Baal followers forgot that as, it seems, have many in our day. Elijah challenged them: "How long will you go limping with two different opinions? If the Lord is God, follow him; but if Baal, then follow him" (1 Kings 18:21). You will note that they had no answer to Elijah's question. Nor, do the pseudo-intellectuals of our generation.

III. The God Who Calls Us To Choose

Today, in this service, we also come to the moment of choice. It is not a choice about whether we will serve, but about whom we will serve for we are already in service to someone. "I call heaven and earth to witness against you today that I have set before you life and death, blessings and curses. Choose life so that you and your descendants may live" (Deuteronomy 30:19).

In the Amazon there is a slave-making ant that illustrates our predicament. Hundreds of these little creatures periodically swarm out of their nest to capture neighboring colonies of weaker ants. They attack with no warning and kill off any defenders before carrying off cocoons containing the larvae of worker ants. When these slave children hatch, they assume they are part of the family around them and launch into the work they were captured to do. They never realize that they are, in fact, forced-labor victims of the enemy. Just as these little ants are bound from the time of birth, so we also enter this world as slaves to sin and Satan. For us, however, there is a solution, and it is to decide resolutely now for Jesus Christ, the Son of God who took away our sins on Calvary's cross. Make your decision for Christ and ask him in the Holy Spirit's power to help you to serve the true God alone for this day and forever more.

What kind of God will you believe in? Which one will you serve? In the name Almighty God, I urge you today to meet the only God who died for you and who alone can make you promises that are good for you and will never be broken. Let this be your day to commit yourself anew to God and to his Son, Jesus, the Lord of the cross.

---

1. Strauss, William and Neil Howe, *The Fourth Turning: An American Prophecy* (New York: Broadway Books, 1998).

Proper 5 • Pentecost 3 • Ordinary Time 10

Secondhand Religion

1 Kings 17:8-24

The life of Elijah is filled with fascinating experiences that help us to see God more clearly and live on a higher plane. Today's Scripture reading is a good example of that. In a nation whose laws required its citizens to provide for the prophets, God used saucy, impudent birds noted for their thievery and dirty lifestyle to feed Elijah. "The ravens brought him bread and meat in the morning, and bread and meat in the evening" (1 Kings 17:6). Ravens live off dead carcasses and steal food stored up by other birds and animals. They have no respect for any living creature. They are noisy and among the messiest of all the birds. Even people who like birds usually don't like ravens. Yet, God used ravens to feed Elijah. God can use the undesirable to do good things. Now, he uses a widow, not just any widow but a widow from the home territory of Jezebel against whose immoral lifestyle Elijah had just preached. The application surely has to be that God, who is Lord of all things, sometimes demonstrates his Lordship by providing for his people in ways that they might never expect. He uses things and people we might never dream of finding useful. Always remember, no matter how deep your troubles, how bitter your trials, or how great your needs, God will provide for you, perhaps in ways that decimate the horizons of your imagination. The point is, he always provides. His chosen name is Jehovah Jireh. It means "The eternal God will provide your needs."

Thomas Chisholm's splendid hymn, "Great Is Thy Faithfulness," has a refrain that comforts and assures us when times are tough:

Morning by Morning new mercies I see:
All I have needed thy hand hath provided.
Great is thy faithfulness, Lord, unto me.[1]

God's faithfulness is great. What is more, it is constant and it is certain. He promises us through Saint Paul, "My God will fully satisfy every need of yours according to his riches in glory in Christ Jesus" (Philippians 4:19). Our Scripture begins at that point in Elijah's life where, having seen God's faithfulness revealed once by the ravens at Brook Kerith, he hears God direct his way once more. "Then the word of the Lord came to him, saying, 'Go now to Zarephath, which belongs to Sidon, and live there; for I have commanded a widow there to feed you' " (1 Kings 17:8, 9). Faith is not measured by how we live in prosperity but by how we honor God in adversity. Let's look at the three major issues presented here.

I. The Widow's Wits' End

She is preparing a last meal, "I have nothing baked." Her possessions are skimpy, to say the least: "Only a handful of meal in a jar, and a little oil in a jug." She has no idea that God has big plans for her.

God instructs Elijah, "I have commanded a widow there to feed you" (1 Kings 17:9). Scripture teaches us that God has a special interest in widows. "Protector of widows is God in his holy habitation" (Psalm 68:5). Yet, here it looks, at least at first, as though God is not going to give this widow life's basic necessities. Rather his initial plan seems to call for Elijah to eat from the meager possessions the widow is planning to use for a final meal.

There is another thing about this widow and it is that she has a secondhand God. Look at what she says to Elijah, "As the Lord your God lives" (1 Kings 17:12). She refers to God as Elijah's God. *"Your God,"* she calls him. Amazingly, we can discern from the text that she believes in God, that is, she gives intellectual assent to Elijah's God. She calls him, "The Lord your God." Not only is he Elijah's God to her, he is, "The Lord." Yet, she has no firsthand experience or relationship with God. She has, as I said, "secondhand religion." Jesus had something to say about people like that: "Many will say to me, 'Lord, Lord, did we not prophesy in your name, and cast out demons in your name, and do many deeds of power in your name?' Then I will declare to them, 'I never knew you; go away from me, you evildoers' " (Matthew 7:23-24). It is possible to know about God, to acknowledge there is a God, to believe who he is and what he has done, and yet not be saved.

A friend of mine registered for his first doctoral-level class at a major seminary in the southeast. As part of the opening exercise, members of the class were asked to introduce themselves and say a few words about their personal faith and why they were interested in studying doctoral level theology. One minister of almost twenty years, said, "Frankly, I'm looking for a faith like my mother had." It is not enough to have a faith like our mother or like our neighbor. The faith the Bible calls us to is always personal, firsthand faith.

Let me say that another way: You may come to church and sit among Christians. You may even be married to a Christian and not be numbered among the ranks of believers because your god, like the widow's, is secondhand. That does not mean you are "bad." You are perhaps no worse than some Christians sitting around you. What it does mean is that you have not trusted Jesus Christ for yourself in a personal relationship. The problem with secondhand religion is that it fails when you need it most. Secondhand religion may seem okay when things are going well, but it will leave you feeling inadequate and all alone against the odds of the world when you most need help. Do not settle for a spiritual life that is a secondhand reflection of what another person believes. Take hold of Christ now for yourself. Commit your life to Jesus today. Make him your Lord by personal faith. Today, you can take Christ as Lord and you will receive his forgiveness and righteousness in exchange for your guilt and doubt. "To all who received him, who believed in his name, he gave power to become children of God" (John 1:12).

The widow needed one thing more. She needed sufficient grace. Even Saint Paul needed to learn that when we see God through our problems, the problems always look bigger. On the other hand, when we see our problems through a loving God and Father, God looks bigger and that is how it really is. Seeing your problems through God puts the problems into perspective. Paul had a recurring struggle in his life. He called it his thorn in the flesh and said that he asked the Lord to remove it three times. Finally, the Lord said, "My grace is sufficient for you, for power is made perfect in weakness." With that, the apostle responded, "So, I will boast all the more gladly of my weaknesses, so that the power of Christ may dwell in me" (2 Corinthians 12:9).

"I have nothing baked, only a handful of meal in a jar, and a little oil in a jug; I am now gathering a couple of sticks, so that I may go home and prepare it for myself and my son, that we may eat it, and die" (1 Kings 17:12). She was blinded from her blessings because she was focused on her lack. Are you? In tough times it is easy to become distracted by what we don't have and miss what we do have. The truth is, however, that people who attach their future to what they can see never go very far. When we attach our future to what God sees, we can go on forever. So, let's be sure that we spend our lives "looking to Jesus the pioneer and perfecter of our faith, who for the sake of the joy that was set before him endured the cross, disregarding its shame, and has taken his seat at the right hand of the throne of God. Consider him who endured such hostility against himself from sinners, so that you may not grow weary or lose heart" (Hebrews 12:2, 3).

II. The Prophet's Potent Poise

"Elijah said to her, 'Do not be afraid; go and do as you have said; but first make me a little cake of it and bring it to me, and afterwards make something for yourself and your son. For thus says the Lord the God of Israel: The jar of meal will not be emptied and the jug of oil will not fail until the day that the Lord sends rain on the earth' " (1 Kings 17:13, 14). His response exhibits three faith principles for us.

The first is that faith practices God's promises. That is, it takes God at his word and acts on what he says. Faith is not an ethereal, idealistic thing. It is an active verb. A few years ago, the *San Francisco Chronicle* published a fascinating story about how Russian parliamentary deputies left "a crucial debate on the republic's future" when they learned that priests were distributing free Bibles outside the parliament hall. The politicians jostled in line for a free Bible. A leader of the Russian Bible Society said, "The word of God softens hearts. In our cruel times, it is good to put Bibles in parliamentarians' hands."[2]

Wouldn't it be wonderful if we could awake such an interest in what God says all across America? Tragically we have cheapened the very thing those Russians esteemed so highly. When we read the Bible and apply its message, life is always better, for it finds a solid standard to guide it. Wouldn't it be wonderful if it was said of each of us what is said of Abraham, "No distrust made him waver concerning the promise of God, but he grew strong in his faith as he gave glory to God, being fully convinced that God was able to do what he had promised" (Romans 4:20-21)?

The second faith principle is that faith prioritizes God's preeminence. Elijah told the widow to put God's work first. "Do not be afraid; go and do as you have said; but first make me a little cake of it and bring it to me, and afterwards make something for yourself and your son" (1 Kings 17:13). Where do your priorities lie? When God comes first, everything else falls into its proper place. Jesus said, "Strive first for the kingdom of God and his righteousness, and all these things will be given to you as well" (Matthew 6:33). Look what happened after the widow put God first: "She went and did as Elijah said, so that she as well as he and her household ate for many days" (1 Kings 17:15, 16). God will take care of you if you read his word, believe its promises and put him first.

The third faith principle is that faith portrays God's prowess. That is, faith shows that we truly believe God is in control. He is, indeed, "the Lord" (1 Kings 17:14). The widow was afraid she would go without until she trusted God and found out for herself that he keeps his word. Is your god one who gets threatened by circumstances? Have you noticed how many "Christians" get hyper with every little problem, every troubling news story, and every anti-Christ look-alike? Why do we get afraid? Is it not that, like the widow, our vision gets out of focus because our God is too small? A sovereign God is frightened by nothing. Neither are his citizens, for "the grass withers, the flower fades; but the word of our God will stand forever" (Isaiah 40:8).

III. Our Savior's Steady Supply

"The jar of meal was not emptied, neither did the jug of oil fail, according to the word of the Lord that he spoke by Elijah" (1 Kings 17:16). God always delivers on his word. All that he promised to Elijah and the widow was provided. "My God will fully satisfy every need of yours according to his riches in glory in Christ Jesus" (Philippians 4:19). All that he promises to us will be provided too.

Whose God are you worshiping and serving? Is your faith in this God of heaven real, intimate, and personal? Or, are you still after all these years looking for the faith of your mother or father? Put your trust unreservedly in Jesus Christ who loved you all the way to Calvary's cross and loves you still. If you have never said it before, say to him now, "Lord Jesus, be my God. Give me personal faith to trust you completely and live my life out for you."

When you do, he will!

---

1. Thomas O. Chisholm, from the hymn, "Great Is Thy Faithfulness." (1923). Copyright, 1951, Hope Publishing Company

2. *San Francisco Chronicle,* September 20, 1991, p. A-15; a report titled, "Run on Bibles at Russian Parliament."

Proper 6 • Pentecost 4 • Ordinary Time 11

Bad News From A Good Man!

1 Kings 21:1-21a

There are two facts we all need to remember before we can make any real sense out of life. The first is that God is sovereign and holy, just and loving. The second is that we are not. We are servants, unholy, self-centered, and self-seeking. This Scripture passage is a marvelous illustration of this. You would think that seeing God send fire from heaven would change a corrupt heart every time. That, however, is not the case, as we can see from the life of Ahab and his Jezebel.

I. The Sliding Spiral Of Human Depravity

John D. Rockefeller was the Bill Gates of his generation. After observing the commercial potential of oil production in western Pennsylvania, Rockefeller built his first petroleum refinery near Cleveland, Ohio. His name became synonymous with wealth. Rockefeller bought out his competitors or forced them out of business through tactics that many people considered ruthless and distasteful. He became, far and away, the wealthiest man in the world. Children followed him wherever he walked, clamoring for the dimes he carried around in his pocket as throwaways. Many institutions benefited from his gifts. He did a lot of good for deserving institutions. Yet, his countenance was that of an unhappy man. Once a reporter asked him, "Mr. Rockefeller, how much money does a man need to be happy?" Rockefeller's response was classic. "Always," he said, "just a little bit more than he has!"

How much land does a king need to be happy? King Ahab might have been the Rockefeller or Gates of his generation. He controlled extraordinary wealth and land holdings. Yet, he was not a happy man. He wanted another vineyard. He approached Naboth, the owner of the vineyard, with a proposition: Naboth, for good reasons, had no interest in selling. "Ahab went home resentful and sullen because of what Naboth the Jezreelite had said to him ... He lay down on his bed, turned away his face, and would not eat" (1 Kings 21:4). He sounds like a spoiled brat, does he not? He reminds me of Alexander the Great, who sat and wept because there were no more worlds to conquer. He had it all, yet he had nothing.

Steve Brown writes, "The most unhappy person in the world is not someone who didn't get what he or she wanted. The most unhappy person is the one who got what he or she wanted and then found out it wasn't as wonderful as expected. The secret of a happy life is not to get what you want but to live with what you've got." [1] That's the truth! Too many of us spend our lives centered on what we don't have instead of thanking God for having blessed us so abundantly. One day we wake up and find out that life is in its autumn and we missed the beauty of the summer. What a tragedy!

When it came to net worth, Naboth didn't possess anything like Ahab's great material wealth. Yet, Naboth possessed something Ahab's money could never buy: satisfaction and appreciation for who he was and how far God had brought him. Moreover, he knew that he must not sell it. "The Lord forbid that I should give you my ancestral inheritance" (1 Kings 21:3). Notice his priorities. They'll slip past you if you go too fast. It was not family inheritance that kept Naboth from selling his vineyard. It was something far deeper than that. It was religious principle. "The Lord forbid," he said. Long before, God said, "The land shall not be sold in perpetuity, for the land is mine; with me you are but aliens and tenants" (Numbers 25:23). Naboth is saying, in effect, this is not mine to sell. It belongs to God. It was not the land that was important to Naboth but the principle of inheritance behind it. What principles guide your life? What is more important to you than money or possessions? As Christians we have a book of principles that was designed for our benefit. What place do those principles play in how you do business and live life? Let us learn anew to appreciate those old standards that have stood the test of time and come to us in the Bible.

Will you notice what happens with unresolved covetousness? If Ahab was a spoiled brat, Jezebel was worse. She was a forger. "She wrote letters in Ahab's name and sealed them with his seal; she sent the letters to the elders and the nobles who lived with Naboth in his city" (1 Kings 21:8). She was a manipulator. "She wrote in the letters, 'Proclaim a fast, and seat Naboth at the head of the assembly' " (1 Kings 21:9). She was a fabricator. "Have (two scoundrels) bring a charge against (Naboth) saying, 'You have cursed God and the king' " (1 Kings 21:10). She was a murderer. "Then take (Naboth) out, and stone him to death" (1 Kings 21:13).

That is how sin works if we do not take control of it and stop it. It is conceived in the mind as insatiable desire for that bit more than we have. Next it sets aside all principles and, finally, it brings out the worst in us. Do you see why it is important to recognize the spiral of human depravity? "Oh," you say, "but that is Ahab and Jezebel, and everybody knows their reputation." I would remind you that Ahab and Jezebel were religious people. They were so spiritual one God would not satisfy them. They had many gods called Baals. Yet, when the standards God set did not satisfy them, they just threw God's rules away. My point is that none of us is immune to depravity and its ways. "There is no one who is righteous, not even one" (Romans 3:10). "All have sinned and fall short of the glory of God" (Romans 3:23). Those tendencies to sin that brought down Ahab and Jezebel are resident in all our lives.

II. Sinister News From A Saint

"The word of the Lord came to Elijah the Tishbite, saying, Go down to meet King Ahab of Israel, who rules in Samaria; he is now in the vineyard of Naboth, where he has gone to take possession. You shall say to him, 'Thus says the Lord: Have you killed, and also taken possession?' You shall say to him, 'Thus says the Lord: In the place where dogs licked up the blood of Naboth, dogs will also lick up your blood.' " (1 Kings 21:17-19). This is bad news from a good man.

"Whatever Became of Sin?" A book by that title was a best seller about two decades ago. It spoke to the fact that there was, in the opinion of the author, prominent psychiatrist Karl Menninger, a scarcity of preaching about human iniquity in America's pulpits. One might wonder what Dr. Menninger would think about today's preaching where there is even less preaching from our pulpits about individual sin and responsibility. Of course, there are even some who would ask, "Whatever became of preaching?" So much of what is presented as preaching is "feel-goodism" and pop psychology. We don't want to dwell too long on human sinfulness. We prefer quick-fix solutions and easy instructions.

Is the message of the Bible that God is love and that his love is seen best in the sacrifice of Jesus, his Son, on the cross? Absolutely. Is it that God is merciful? Definitely. But above all else, it is that God is sovereign, just, and holy and that sin demands its price in this life and in the life to come.

Let me ask you a question: Do you believe in any principle so deeply that you would sacrifice your own child for it? God does. For God, the thing more important than preserving his Son's life is the satisfaction of sin's penalty on our account. That penalty, says the Bible, is death.

There is no joy in preaching judgment. Elijah knew that when he apprehended Ahab and Jezebel. He had just experienced a nervous breakdown, a deep spell of personal despondency where he had begged God to allow him to die. Now his assignment was to confront a king and his queen, knowing full well that they would just as soon take off his head as shake his hand. His commission was to confront them where they were wrong in the name of the Lord and tell them that God would bring his wrath upon them. Listen to this verse that keeps many preachers awake at night: "If the sentinel sees the sword coming and does not blow the trumpet, so that the people are not warned, and the sword comes and takes any of them, they are taken away in their iniquity, but their blood I will require at the sentinel's hand" (Ezekiel 33:6). It speaks directly to the sin of omission in the life of a preacher. When we preachers fail to declare the full counsel of God, there is a price to be paid. Elijah must deliver the message faithfully, as must I.

Some years ago in Logan County, West Virginia, a mountain cabin burned to the ground. All that remained was the large stone fireplace and its smoke-blackened chimney. Since the owner wanted to keep people out of the ruins, he painted a sign as a warning and posted it at the edge of what used to be his cabin. It was intended to read, "WARNING — NO TRESPASSING." In his hurry, however, the owner printed, "WARNING — NO TRUSTPASSING." Pastors are "trustpassing" when they fail to declare the whole message of the Bible and preach only one side of God's personality. Elijah recognized that he must first be faithful to God. Like Elijah, I have a God-given obligation to tell you that God judges sin.

III. The Siren Sound Of The Sovereign Savior

"The word of the Lord came to Elijah the Tishbite, saying." God's word sounds forth calling Elijah to action and Ahab to repentance. God always has the last word on sin. "So then, each of us will be accountable to God" (Romans 14:12). Make no mistake; no one escapes this world alive. Every one of us faces the junction of God's eternal judgment. "It is appointed for mortals to die once, and after that the judgment" (Hebrews 9:27). John, on Patmos, writes:

> *I saw a great white throne and the one who sat on it; the earth and the heaven fled from his presence, and no place was found for them. And I saw the dead, great and small, standing before the throne, and books were opened. Also another book was opened, the book of life. And the dead were judged according to their works, as recorded in the books. And the sea gave up the dead that were in it, Death and Hades gave up the dead that were in them, and all were judged according to what they had done. Then Death and Hades were thrown into the lake of fire. This is the second death, the lake of fire; and anyone whose name was not found written in the book of life was thrown into the lake of fire.*
> — Revelation 20:11-15

Let there be no misunderstanding! The final word in history will belong to Almighty Christ. He is loving. He is patient. He is gracious. And he always keeps his word. "Therefore, beloved, while you are waiting for these things, strive to be found by him at peace, without spot or blemish" (2 Peter 3:14).

You ask, "How can I be found at peace with no spot and no blemish when I am a sinner?" The answer is through the loving mercy of God's Son, Jesus. How far different might history have spoken of Ahab and his Jezebel if only they had learned to take God at his word and trust his gracious salvation! "God proves his love for us in that while we still were sinners Christ died for us" (Romans 5:8). We find God's peace and forgiveness through the cross of Jesus. Not in gathering possessions! Not in building power! Only in trusting Jesus, the loving Savior of Calvary's cross.

At the dawning of the Christian era, according to an ancient story, a Roman girl of high birth and culture refused the attention of all the eligible young men who tried to court her. "No man shall ever win my heart," she declared, "unless he first proves that he would die for me." One day, she overheard a group of Christians speaking about the Lord. They spoke of how he formed the universe and how he fulfilled the words of the prophets by coming to earth as a Bethlehem baby. She heard them describe his wonderful message and marvelous example of miracles and parables. She was caught in rapt attention as they told about his crucifixion on the cross that took away our sins. God's Spirit moved in her heart and in amazement she exclaimed, "This is the man I want to give my heart. This is the man who died for me." Today, you can give Christ your heart. Today you can enter the road to happiness. Do not allow this moment to pass you by for Christ's sake and for your own sake.

---

1. Brown, Steve. *Jumping Hurdles, Hitting Glitches, Overcoming Setbacks* (Colorado Springs: Navpress, 1992), p. 150.

Proper 7 • *Pentecost 5* • *Ordinary Time 12*

The Second Touch For The Out Of Touch!

1 Kings 19:1-15a

There's an old legend that tells how God sent one of his angels to Satan with the message that all the methods the devil uses to defeat Christians would be taken from him. The devil pleaded to be allowed to keep only one. The angel, thinking it an unusual, modest request from the greedy devil, agreed Satan could keep that one. "Which one would you want to keep?" the angel inquired. "Let me keep discouragement," was Lucifer's reply. The angel agreed. Satan could keep discouragement. And the devil rejoiced for, said he, "In this one I have secured all I shall ever need to accomplish my dastardly work."

Have you ever felt discouraged? Have you been at the point where you believed your best had already been? Have you experienced that miserable, wretched sickness of the spirit that leaves you feeling useless, uninvolved, and in deep, hopeless despair? Do you know that feeling that leaves you wondering if God is through with you? If you have not been there, the chances are you will. Almost all of us experience spiritual depression at one time or another in our lives. It seems to be part and parcel of the normal human experience.

Until now Elijah's life was uniquely marked by success. Everything he put his hand to seemed to prosper. When it seemed as though he should have been riding the crest of the wave, depression entered his life, proving that James was right when he said, "Elijah was a human being like us" (James 5:17). A woman in his congregation asked one of my preacher friends what accounted for Elijah's depression. "How come," she wanted to know, "there was this sudden change from the bold prophet of God on Mount Carmel to the fearful man who fled from Jezebel and whimpered out a prayer request for death to come quickly?" It was a good question. At first glance it does seem rather strange that a man who rebuked a king, challenged 450 Baal prophets on Mount Carmel, and called down fire from heaven should become so discouraged. Yet, he did! When you think about it for a bit, it's not as unusual as we might believe. You can be sure that Elijah's adrenaline was flowing freely when he was on the mountain and as he ran those seventeen miles into Jezreel. He was ripe for an emotional collapse. When Jezebel warned him what she planned to do, his mind went into park and his feelings took over, causing him to panic and want to die. Blinded by emotion, he was persuaded that his victory on Mount Carmel was of no account. His negative thoughts coupled with exhaustion coming off his powerful victory caused him to fall into a deep depression. Some of you will identify with that. You have been there. Perhaps you are now. If that is the case, God has a wonderful word for you today. Let's think about Elijah's experience and see what God has in store.

I. Elijah's Dilapidated Condition

"He asked that he might die: 'It is enough; now, O Lord, take away my life, for I am no better than my ancestors' " (1 Kings 19:4). Have you ever "had enough"? Not long ago a friend of mine was leading a church retreat. It was attended by a number of young families from the church. One young woman had to go alone because her husband, who had just had major surgery, was unable to get any more time off work and go with her. Late one evening, her misbehaving children seemed to be out of control. Suddenly she screamed, "I'm a woman on the edge!" It was a cry for help that I suspect is being made by many young mothers in our high-pressure world.

Elijah was on the edge. He was frightened. "He was afraid" (1 Kings 19:3). He wanted to be left alone. "He left his servant there" (1 Kings 19:3). One of depression's primary symptoms is the desire for aloneness. Then, often when we are left alone, we crave company! He was detached from reality and caught in a web of ambivalence: "He got up and fled for his life" (1 Kings 19:3). Twice, it says, he had a sense that he stood alone against the world: "I have been very zealous for the Lord, the God of hosts (and) ... I alone am left, and they are seeking my life, to take it away" (1 Kings 19:10, 14).

"I'm the only one who stands for righteousness!" Have you ever thought that? "Mine is the only right way!" Have you ever been persuaded of that? Yet, notice that he ran away. If he was so certain he was right, why did he leave? I'll tell you why: it was because he was depressed and his words and true belief (which were betrayed by his actions) were conflicted against each other. That weariness that leads to deep depression often reveals itself in a martyr complex. "So if you think you are standing, watch out that you do not fall" (1 Corinthians 10:12). "My friends, if anyone is detected in a transgression, you who have received the Spirit should restore such a one in a spirit of gentleness. Take care that you yourselves are not tempted" (Galatians 6:1). Are you listening? Is this your life described in Elijah's experience?

Let me take it one step further: Will you notice the preeminence of the first personal pronoun? "I alone." "I have been very zealous for the Lord." "I alone am left." His reality begins with himself. The truth is that our reality never begins with us. It always begins with God, whether we realize it or not. To assess life without factoring in God's proper place is to measure it with a defective base of reality. When we take our role too seriously we are in trouble. Elijah was going through what the old family doctors called a nervous breakdown. Life was getting on top of him and it was too heavy for him to bear. Now, notice three key factors that brought Elijah to this point. In seeing them you may be saved from a similar disaster.

II. Elijah's Dire Consequences

"It is enough," he said (1 Kings 19:4). *The New International Version* captures his emotion more realistically, "I've had *enough!*" Elijah had all he could take. Death seemed more attractive than life for him. Many systems are involved in being human. The Bible focuses principally on three: body, mind, and spirit. The Apostle Paul, for example, writes, "May the God of peace himself sanctify you entirely; and may your spirit and soul and body be kept sound and blameless at the coming of our Lord Jesus Christ" (1 Thessalonians 5:23). Each affects the other, and all of them interplayed in Elijah's breakdown. Christian discipleship has something to say about each area of our lives that can help us avoid Elijah's predicament, which I believe was emotional, as opposed to chemical, depression.

His body was depleted. Elijah was physically fatigued. For three and one half years his body took the abuse of drought and dusty conditions. No water meant nothing to drink. It also meant no bathing. His filthy body was likely a haven for all manner of disease. Following a period of intense pressure he walked eighteen miles from Carmel to Beersheba. It was a journey that would exhaust a healthy person under the best of circumstances. The Bible says, "The body is meant not for fornication but for the Lord, and the Lord for the body ... Do you not know that your body is a temple of the Holy Spirit within you, which you have from God, and that you are not your own?" (1 Corinthians 6:13, 19). Take care of your body. It belongs to God.

His mind was depleted. Elijah was physically fatigued. He was also mentally frazzled. There is a mental drain to preaching that is best understood by those who are called to do it regularly. Someone described it as delivering a new paper on the same subject once every seven days. Winston Churchill said, "Any man who believes he can hold the attention of the same audience week after week while he speaks to the same subject is a fool!" He was right in one sense, for even the Bible calls it "the foolishness of preaching" (1 Corinthians 1:21). Yet, the same Bible also says that it is through this foolishness called preaching that God saves believers. There is tension that comes from daily standing at the front of this battle for the souls of our generation. Every herald of Christ knows it, and many drop out of the ministry because they can no longer stand the strain. There is tension, too, for you where you serve Christ. You have learned, have you not, that the enemy of the cross on which Christ died never retreats? "Be on your guard, so that you do not lose what we have worked for" (2 John 1:8). Spiritual diligence demands a heavy psychological price, as well as being physically fatiguing.

His spirit was depleted. He was spiritually fractured. "I alone am left, and they are seeking my life" (1 Kings 19:10). He forgot that he was never alone. His Lord says, "I will never leave you or forsake you" (Hebrews 13:5). Always remember this: When you belong to Jesus you are never the last one. Elijah took his eyes off God and paid homage to Queen Jezebel and all her wicked ways. Courage was replaced with cowardice. Faith was superseded by fear. Do you feel disconnected from God? Do you sense that somehow you are out of touch with heaven? Is it not because you have looked away from Jesus?

Depression often sets in when we allow ourselves to be physically fatigued, mentally frazzled, and spiritually fractured. We need to remember this:

III. There's A Second Touch For The Out Of Touch

God's gentle whisper came to Elijah's troubled soul.

The text describes it as "a sound of sheer silence" (1 Kings 19:12). Elijah was learning that this God, who once spoke by fire that consumed a soaked altar sacrifice, does not always reveal himself in powerful, miraculous visionary ways. Some people think that the only place to find God is in something big. They hunt out the biggest churches, follow the crowd to the largest conferences, and consult highly-visible Christian leaders. Certainly God is found in those places too. Yet, I submit to you, that God is more often found gently whispering in the quietness of a trusting heart. Are you listening for God's voice? Come away to a quiet place where he can speak to you alone in his special kind of silence.

> *He speaks, and the sound of his voice*
> *Is so sweet the birds hush their singing,*
> *And the melody that he gave to me*
> *Within my heart is ringing.*
> *And he walks with me,*
> *And he talks with me,*
> *And he tells me I am his own,*

*And the joy we share as we tarry there,
None other has ever known.*[1]

This God who came for Elijah in a new way is here today looking for you. Just as he brought Elijah a new touch and a new lease on life, so for you he brings the same.

Elijah, once physically fatigued, found food and rest for his weary body.

> *He lay down under the broom tree and fell asleep. Suddenly an angel touched him and said to him, "Get up and eat." He looked, and there at his head was a cake baked on hot stones, and a jar of water. He ate and drank, and lay down again. The angel of the Lord came a second time, touched him, and said, 'Get up and eat, otherwise the journey will be too much for you.' He got up, and ate and drank; then he went in the strength of that food forty days and forty nights to Horeb the mount of God.* — 1 Kings 19:5-8

Elijah, once mentally frazzled, found renewal for his mind. Two times God asked him a question: "What are you doing here, Elijah?" (1 Kings 19:9, 13). God's repeated question called Elijah to face his life's most basic value. "What are you about?" What is your life's mission? Is it to accumulate wealth, power, prestige, fame? Is that all there is to you? No! Surely not! You were born to enjoy fellowship with God and serve him with your life. Come back to the basics. What are you doing? Why are you doing it? Bring your thinking back to God.

Elijah, once spiritually fractured, detached from God, found reunion. God came looking. "Go out and stand on the mountain before the Lord, for the Lord is about to pass by" (1 Kings 19:11). Listen for the sound of the silence, the voice that speaks to a quieted heart and reminds you that God's love for you has never failed. Don't give up when depression comes. Don't be a spiritual has-been. "The Lord said to him, 'Go, return on your way' " (1 Kings 19:15). It's another way of saying to Elijah and to you and me, "Go back the way you came." And the way we came was through Jesus,

God's one and only begotten Son, who says, "I am the way, and the truth, and the life" (John 14:6).

There is a second touch for the out of touch, and a third, and a fourth ... There's another touch for you today if you need it.

---

1. C. Austin Miles, "I Come to the Garden Alone," copyright 1940, (New York: The Rodehaver Company).

Proper 8 • Pentecost 6 • Ordinary Time 13

One Fired-Up Preacher!

2 Kings 2:1-2, 6-14

Norval Christy was fifteen years old when he agreed with the Lord that everything he possessed was a gift and that he was willing to use it in God's service however, whenever, and wherever God chose. After attending Westminster College in Pennsylvania, Norval applied to Harvard Medical School and was accepted in spite of long odds. He was in the process of doing his medical residency when a call came to help the thousands of refugees who were flooding into Pakistan from India. Norval agreed to interrupt his post-graduate medical training for six months to assist them. Little did he or his wife Dorothy know that their initial six-month commitment to serve the Lord would end up being 51 years on the foreign mission field in Pakistan and the Orient. Nor did they know that along the way he would practice surgery, orthopedics, obstetrics, and ophthalmology, eventually becoming one of the most respected eye surgeons in the world. During those 51 years, Dr. Christy performed more than 100,000 cataract operations in a land where most of the people are not Christians but where every patient of his heard about and saw the love of Christ in action. There really is no telling what God will do with a willing servant. Today, as they encourage other Christians to consider serving overseas in Christian mission, the Christys rejoice that God used them in ways they had never imagined.

What a way to go! Elijah, having experienced defeat and depression after the Mount Carmel challenge, was restored to greatness in a way he could have never imagined. Without dying, he was caught up to heaven in a whirlwind on a chariot of fire. None of us may expect to go that way but all of us can learn some valuable lessons from Elijah's homegoing. There are three things I want us to see in our Scripture reading.

I. First, there is a life to come and we should prepare for it.

"As they continued walking and talking, a chariot of fire and horses of fire separated the two of them, and Elijah ascended in a whirlwind into heaven" (2 Kings 2:11). C. S. Lewis writes for children, "People do find it hard to keep on feeling as if you believed in the next life: but then it is just as hard to keep on feeling as if you believed you were going to be nothing after death. I know this because in the old days before I was a Christian I used to try."[1] Lewis came to see that reason itself denies that veil, which we in our ignorance call death, is the end of our existence. If we were made to live only thirty, forty, seventy, ninety, 100 years in this life developing our personality and prodigy to be snuffed out like a candle in the wind, life truly would be the final futility. Peggy Lee's haunting lyrics would make a good hymn: "If that's all there is, my friends, then let's keep dancing, bring out the booze and have a ball. If that's all...." But, rest assured, this is not all. Saint Paul writes, "If for this life only we have hoped in Christ, we are of all people most to be pitied" (1 Corinthians 15:19).

For this reason we say with confidence that death is not the end but a pathway. It is not a state but an act, not a condition but a channel and not the grave but a graduation into glory. Everybody's favorite Psalm speaks of walking "through the darkest valley," not of being caught in it. Moreover, you will recall that David, the psalmist, says that when that moment comes he will "fear no evil; for you are with me; your rod and your staff — they comfort me" (Psalm 23:4). What a wonderful idea: We flash from this dark world into the world of unending light. Death for Christians is not a dark passage but a bridge of smiles. Because of the cross where Jesus put death to death for us, we can say these things with confidence. "Yes, we do have confidence, and we would rather be away from the body and at home with the Lord" (2 Corinthians 5:8).

But, Elijah went to heaven without dying! "Elijah ascended in a whirlwind into heaven." Isn't it amazing! Does it sound far-fetched?

Mysterious? It is, in fact, no farther fetched nor mysterious than your death or mine. "Listen, I will tell you a mystery! We will not all die, but we will all be changed" (1 Corinthians 15:51).

> *For this we declare to you by the word of the Lord, that we who are alive, who are left until the coming of the Lord, will by no means precede those who have died. For the Lord himself, with a cry of command, with the archangel's call and with the sound of God's trumpet, will descend from heaven, and the dead in Christ will rise first. Then we who are alive, who are left, will be caught up in the clouds together with them to meet the Lord in the air; and so we will be with the Lord forever.* — 1 Thessalonians 4:15-17

> *This grace was given to us in Christ Jesus before the ages began, but it has now been revealed through the appearing of our Savior Christ Jesus, who abolished death and brought life and immortality to light through the gospel.* — 2 Timothy 1:9, 10

God, who came to earth in Jesus to redeem us, has done something unimaginably wonderful with death.

Let me tell you that not only is there a life to come ...

II. Second, there is a life to live and we should go for it.

"The Lord has sent me as far as Bethel" ... "The Lord has sent me to Jericho"... "The Lord has sent me to the Jordan" (cf., 2 Kings 2:2, 4, 6). Have you ever felt brokenhearted, alone, or despondent? Elijah knew all those feelings too. Not long before, perhaps you remember, Elijah prayed to die. "It is enough; now, O Lord, take away my life" (1 Kings 19:4). It was the only petition in his prayer not answered. I can imagine that as he swept towards heaven on that chariot, he was cheering God and crying out, "Thank you, Lord, for not answering every prayer the way I asked it." He had recovered from his depression and found a new mission from God in Bethel, Jericho, and the Jordan. Are you waiting for God to answer your prayer? Could it be that God has already sent his answer in a way you have not yet recognized? Don't sit around waiting. If God wants to tap us for special service, he is more likely to call on us if we're busy at our daily task than if we're waiting for an angel to ring the doorbell. Norval Christy saw the need and offered to help meet it. He could see that there was work to do. Get on with what needs to be done around you and God will direct your paths.

The essence of Christian maturity comes with the realization that God through his Son Jesus has connected us to a life that is bigger than today. We can easily become entangled by the snare of this moment, by our dreams, our plans, our will and we miss the better way, the way of God for us. When we try to fit God into our idea of what is best we often fail to capture his plans for us. That is a sign of immaturity. In the world of the spirit we can be young once but immature forever. Some people have walked with Christ for years. They were children of the church but somehow their Christian growth was stunted at an early stage. To be spiritually immature is to want God on your own terms instead of his terms. It is to be so focused on today and yesterday that we miss the vision God has for tomorrow. To be a mature Christian, on the other hand, is to want to build churches where you may never worship. It is to be committed to the idea that the greatest mission outreach program of the church is yet to happen. It is to believe with all your heart that the best preacher this congregation will ever have is still to come. It is to be persuaded that the best youth group our church will ever have is yet to be formed and the best Christian Education program we will have is yet to be developed, and to give yourself to making these things happen. Once Elijah believed his life was all over, but God had a far bigger plan for Elijah. The same God has bigger plans for us too.

"Elijah took his mantle and rolled it up, and struck the water; the water was parted to the one side and to the other, until the two of them crossed on dry ground" (2 Kings 2:8). "(Elisha) took the mantle of Elijah that had fallen from him, and struck the water, saying, 'Where is the Lord, the God of Elijah?' When he had struck the water, the water was parted to the one side and to the other, and Elisha went over" (2 Kings 2:14). Elijah's cloak was his symbol of his authority as God's prophet for that time. That dividing of the water so impressed young Elisha that he pleaded with God to do it again and confirm that he really was Elijah's successor. The point is that God was into something far bigger than Elijah. God has bigger plans for your life and for mine. His plan is so big it is bigger than all of us. Don't get so caught up with the past or with this moment or you will miss that.

A career army officer delivered his report on the state of military readiness to former General and then President Dwight Eisenhower. As he finished his report, the officer, recognizing some of its failings, attempted to excuse his performance and flatter the President by recalling "the good old days." "You know, Mr. President," he said, "things will just never be as good as they were in the old brown shoe army." Eisenhower realized that the "good old days" have a way of growing a halo with times passing. He replied, "I know. And they never were!"

The same is true in God's army, the church. As long as we try to recapture what used to be or try to hold on to what we have, we miss God's best plans for the future. Elijah learned that lesson and went about his mission of making ready for the future God intended.

One night a friend of mine was driving a new widow home from the nursing home where her husband had just died. As they came off a side street onto a major thoroughfare, the widow said, "The traffic just keeps going as though nothing has happened." It was a natural comment for a widow to make in that setting. Her world had stalled for a minute. Life would be different from now on. Yet, she was facing the fact that the world keeps on going. That is never more true than when we invest our lives in furthering the kingdom of Christ on earth. Elijah's time was over, but Elisha's time was just beginning.

Not only does this reading teach us that there is a life to come and we should prepare for it and that there is a life to live and we should go for it. It teaches us ...

III. Third, there is a death to die and we should live for it.

Even though he did not die, Elijah teaches us three practical life principles we can apply in preparing for our death. The first is that we should make ourselves busy in God's business, expanding his kingdom. "The Lord has sent me as far as Bethel" ... "The Lord has sent me to Jericho"... "The Lord has sent me to the Jordan" (cf., 2 Kings 2:2, 4, 6). What a ministry! As the end drew near, Elijah stayed busy paving the way for his successor. In a course on geriatrics, a seminary professor assigned his students a paper titled, "A Biblical Plan for Retirement." He added, "Anybody who writes this paper will fail the course!" He went on to tell them that although the Bible has a great deal to say about aging and death, it says nothing about retirement from God's work. It does, however, have something to say about "refirement," that is, the idea of refocusing our lives more fully into God's business.

The second principle Elijah teaches us is that we must keep the faith in the face of death. "Elijah took his mantle and rolled it up, and struck the water; the water was parted to the one side and to the other, until the two of them crossed on dry ground" (2 Kings 2:8). Just before he died, Elijah exercised faith as real as he had done that day on Mount Carmel when the fire fell from heaven. His faith produced another miracle. Yours can too if you keep on practicing it.

The third principle Elijah teaches us about living in the face of death is that we should plan to leave a blessing behind. "Elijah said to Elisha, 'Tell me what I may do for you, before I am taken from you'" (2 Kings 2:9). What might we leave that will bless the generation that takes up God's work after we are gone? Do it! The best is still to be. Invest your life in the next generation and put God's work in your will, and you will be a part of God's plan for tomorrow.

"Elijah ascended in a whirlwind into heaven" (2 Kings 2:11). Will you? Oh, maybe not in a whirlwind. But will you go to heaven? You can know for sure that you will if you are trusting God's Son, Jesus.

---

1. C. S. Lewis, *Letters to Children,* edited by Lyle W. Dorsett and Marjorie Lamp Mead, (New York: Macmillan, 1985), p. 61.

Proper 9 • *Pentecost 7* • *Ordinary Time 14*

The ABC Gospel

2 Kings 5:1-14

Someone has called it ABC spirituality, meaning, "Anything But Christianity." In the search for religious meaning, our generation seems to have a limitless imagination. Past-life regressions, out-of-body experiences, channeling, mantras — the list goes on and on. The New Age (which is truly just old Hinduism warmed over), Zen yoga, seances — anything but faith in the resurrected Lord of the cross.

Today's Scripture reading has a character like that. His name is Naaman. Of all the stories connected with the life of Elisha, the story of Naaman is probably the best known. Although it happened long ago, it has some striking parallels for our own experience. As we think of Naaman, we can begin to see that we could very well put ourselves in this picture. Instead of Naaman's name, we could insert our own name. Instead of leprosy, we could insert some of the diseases prevalent in our generation such as cancer or AIDS or even the universal plague that afflicts us all, a sinful nature. In the place of the River Jordan, we could substitute Calvary where John says, "The blood of Jesus his Son cleanses us from all sin" (1 John 1:7). Consider three things we see in this Scripture passage.

I. The Man, Naaman

"Naaman, commander of the army of the king of Aram, was a great man and in high favor with his master, because by him the Lord had given victory to Aram. The man, though a mighty warrior, suffered from leprosy" (2 Kings 5:1). Some people live a long life and die without seeming to accomplish anything worth noting.

Others seem to possess a charisma that takes them quickly to fame and following. They make a name for themselves that attracts others like a magnet. Naaman was like that. Wherever he went he stood head and shoulders against the crowd. He was an achiever. Look at some of the superlatives from this one-verse introduction. He was a commander of the army of the king of Aram. He was a great man. He was a high favorite with his master. He was a winner: "The Lord had given victory to Aram." He was a mighty warrior. Naaman was a leader in the sight of his people and his king. Moreover, he was a man with God's touch on his life. Everybody knew that God had used Naaman to bring victory in battle.

When we have said all these things about Naaman, however, we have also left something very important unsaid. Naaman's life, blessed as it was, was not perfect. "The man ... suffered from leprosy." Beneath the splendor of his erect posture, this highly-decorated man carried a story of tragedy and great sorrow. Underneath the magnificence was a disease which, unless there were a miracle, would most likely finally bring Naaman low and take his life.

Leprosy, much like AIDS today, was one of the most-feared diseases of its time. It was not well understood, a fact that brought some special stigmas with it. It came in many forms, some of which were known to be highly contagious and all of which were highly visible. We have all seen pictures of lepers with parts of their bodies eaten away by this disease. Because it is a disease of this nature, in Bible times as the disease progressed, lepers were usually consigned to quarantined colonies. There, separated from family and friends, lepers lived out their days watching each other suffer and die. Often the Bible uses leprosy as a sort of synonym for sin. The implication is that both are highly contagious, destructive, and lead to death.

Are you getting the picture? Perhaps now you begin to identify more with this man Naaman. His leprosy would eat away his exterior. Maybe yours eats away at your inner being, your soul. There is sin in your heart, perhaps a memory of long ago, and you fear that if people knew they would shut you off from the society you know. You live with the haunting possibility that one day it will be found out. This is the picture of thousands, perhaps millions, of people in our society. It is the reason why many people spend valuable time in psychiatrists' offices. To the world around them, they seem to be wonderful people, decent and moral. They are sometimes leaders in their communities, yet they are eaten up with sin. Like Naaman, they are wonderful people, but they have this one nagging flaw that they fear might bring about their destruction. If this is your life, I have good news for you today. Before I tell you what it is, let me tell you a bit more about the Bible text.

II. The Maid, Unnamed

"Now the Arameans on one of their raids had taken a young girl captive from the land of Israel, and she served Naaman's wife. She said to her mistress, 'If only my lord were with the prophet who is in Samaria! He would cure him of his leprosy.' So Naaman went in and told his lord just what the girl from the land of Israel had said'" (2 Kings 2:2-4). Aram was Israel's northeastern neighbor, and the two nations were constantly at war with one another. During the time of Naaman and Elisha, Aram was on an expansion program. The Arameans often conducted raids on Israel and took captives who would become slaves to the leaders of their society. This young woman was such a person. She was captured from a background in Israel that had brought her up in the ways of God. Even in her captivity she had held onto him, trusting him and bearing witness to his power to do great things. When she learned that her master and captor was a leper, she set aside all the prejudices and bitterness she might have had because of her capture and tried to help him find a cure. She told his wife about the power of God who could bring healing to her husband's life. Who would have ever guessed it?

"Do not neglect to show hospitality to strangers, for by doing that some have entertained angels without knowing it" (Hebrews 13:2). One stormy night a country doctor in Wales was called to help deliver a child. The weather was so bad it was dangerous to venture outside. Knowing that the family was too poor even to pay his fee, the doctor contemplated refusing to answer the patient's urgent appeal. Yet, he knew that there was a good possibility of complications. Disregarding his personal comfort and safety, he set out to brave the furious elements. It was well he did, for indeed there were complications and without his help the child who was born that night probably would have died. Later, near the end of his life, that Welsh country doctor recalled that he had no idea that night that he was saving the life of one of his country's future great leaders. Those poor parents called their son David Lloyd George. He grew to become one of the greatest prime ministers and statesmen in British history.

We have no way of knowing what plans God has for the people around us. Who would have ever guessed that this young captive Jewish girl was, in fact, an agent of God for good in Naaman's life, an angel unaware? Three other Old Testament personalities "entertained angels without knowing it." They were Abraham (in Genesis chapter 18), Gideon (in Judges chapter 6) and Manoah (in Judges chapter 13). Have you ever entertained an angel unawares? Are there ever visitors at your church who might enjoy an invitation to coffee after the service? Are there elderly people who might enjoy a visit? Perhaps there is a young person who could use help and guidance in dealing with the struggles of youth, and you might just be the agent God intends to meet them at their point of need. You might be their angel unawares.

Naaman might have looked impressive in the sight of all his people, but to this young maid he was a man with a desperate need that only God could meet. She spoke of God's amazing power to heal even those diseases science calls hopeless. Naaman was at first inclined to reject the prescription that came to him. He failed to understand the way God works with us. "He went, taking with him ten talents of silver, six thousand shekels of gold, and ten sets of garments" (2 Kings 5:5). Naaman wanted to buy the cure! He failed to understand that God always enters our lives as an act of grace. His power is not for sale. "He brought the letter to the king of Israel, which read, 'When this letter reaches you, know that I have sent to you my servant Naaman, that you may cure him of his leprosy' " (2 Kings 5:6). Now he wanted to use his political influence. He looked to the King of Israel for a cure instead of the King of kings. Even when he finally met Elisha, he still wanted to follow his own way:

> *Elisha sent a messenger to him, saying, "Go, wash in the Jordan seven times, and your flesh shall be restored and you shall be clean." But Naaman became angry and went away, saying, "I thought that for me he would surely come out, and stand and call on the name of the Lord his God, and would wave his hand over the spot, and cure the leprosy!"* — 2 Kings 5:10-11

How often have we done that? We know that God in heaven has the answers to the situations in which we find ourselves, yet we refuse to cooperate with him to do what needs to be done. Naaman wanted God's healing, but he wanted it on his own terms. How many times have we done that? It was only after his staff pleaded with him that Naaman surrendered to God's leadership.

III. The Miracle: Healing For Naaman!

In the end Naaman was forced to acknowledge that the only way really to find healing was God's way. No matter how much money and goods Naaman could gather, it would never be sufficient. No matter how much political pull Naaman had, it would never be enough. No matter how stubborn he might have been, God's way would have to prevail or there would be no healing. His servants spoke earnestly to him: "His servants approached and said to him, 'Father, if the prophet had commanded you to do something difficult, would you not have done it? How much more, when all he said to you was, "Wash, and be clean" '?" (2 Kings 5:13). It was, first, a maiden of his house who directed him to Israel. Now it was his servants who brought about his submission to Elisha's instructions.

Naaman was humbled: "He went down" (2 Kings 5:14). Naaman was obedient: "(He) immersed himself seven times in the Jordan, according to the word of the man of God." Naaman was healed. "His flesh was restored like the flesh of a young boy, and he was clean." Another way to read that is that Naaman became a whole new man. Real healing came not only on the outside but also on the inside.

"So if anyone is in Christ, there is a new creation: everything old has passed away; see, everything has become new!" (2 Corinthians 5:17). Almost unbelievable is the transformation that occurs when Christ is given full access to a person's heart. In his *Collected Essays*, English author Augustine Birrell tells about traveling into what was, at the time, a wild, remote part of Lancashire where the people had a reputation for being pugnacious, heavy drinkers, and fighters. When Birrell visited that area, he found its people to be about as far removed from their reputation as he could have imagined. Finally, in a conversation with a local coal miner, Augustine Birrell said what he had heard and the contrast he had found. The man responded in a way that was temperate and kind, acknowledging that what he heard was once a fact. "What happened?" Birrell asked the miner. The man tipped his hat as a mark of respect and replied, "There came among us once a man whose name was John Wesley and we have not been the same since." The testimony of John Wesley had impacted a whole community for Jesus Christ.

Imagine what might happen where we live if once again people could see the positive difference Jesus makes to all who follow him completely! What a transformation! What a powerful change! It can happen. It will happen as we surrender completely, as did Naaman, to everything that God calls us to be and do. May it begin to happen here and now for Christ's sake as well as for our sakes.

Proper 10 • *Pentecost 8* • *Ordinary Time 15*

Plumb Line Prophecy

Amos 7:7-17

Not many tourists to Washington, D.C., look for the Federal Bureau of Standards offices. It's the Capitol and the White House, the Supreme Court Building or the Smithsonian most of us want to see when we go there. Yet, at the Bureau of Standards offices something very important is stored, something that impacts your life and mine every single day. Have you ever bought the materials for a new project? When you did, most likely you purchased so many inches or feet or yards. Or, you stopped to buy gasoline for your car and purchased it at a certain price per gallon. Just what is an inch, foot, or yard anyway, or a gallon or millimeter or milligram? It is a nationally-accepted standard of measurement, the perfect example of which is stored intact at the Federal Bureau of Standards in the nation's capital. Every weight and measure we have finds its final proof in those offices, and all are judged by the perfect measurements that are stored under protection there.

Amos did not come from the capital city. He was a herdsman and fig farmer from the farm country south of Judah. But he knew a false measurement when he saw one. The nation of Israel was intoxicated with optimism — but it was optimism based on false standards. The people were happy. They had plenty of money, nice homes, beds carved of ivory, and lives of leisure. Business was booming and national boundaries were expanding, but it was all a façade based on false confidence. Behind it, there was spiritual rot at the nation's heart. Spiritually and morally the people of Israel were rotting away at the center. Amos could see it. He knew counterfeit security from the real thing. God called Amos to take the message of impending judgment to the nation's capital. It was a heady assignment for a country preacher, but one he had no choice about accepting. Time after time in his prophecy he told the Israelites how they were measuring success by false standards. He warned them about the consequences of not returning to that which has validity, but the people paid no heed. It is no wonder he was not popular.

God gave Amos three visions of judgment. In the first, a swarm of locusts would come to devour Israel's crops unless the people returned to their religious roots. In the second, a fire would come and leave their beautiful cities lying in rubble. In each case the people were unmoved by the message. Amos didn't like to be a bad news bearer (what preacher does?) and he begged God to relent and spare the people. God heard him and held back the judgment of locusts and fire. Now, God came with a third and final prophecy vision for Amos. The first two threats took the form of utter ruin through an unstoppable disaster, an act of God. The third vision Amos had was not so much a judgment as a measurement of where they were spiritually. God said he would send a plumb line to demonstrate the spiritual state of the nation. "I am setting a plumb line in the midst of my people Israel" (Amos 7:8).

What is a plumb line? It is a weight suspended from a line for fixing or measuring vertical direction. Most often it is used to determine the straightness of walls. It can also be used to measure the depth of water. A plumb line is not a judgment but a test. It tells whether a wall is really true or not. When a builder wants to check his work, he uses a plumb line to see if it's true to the vertical. A plumb line's greatest strength is that it never fails. It is as certain as the law of gravity by which it works. This spiritual plumb line would measure whether or not the Israelites were truly upright. It would measure the true depth of their commitment to God and expose just how shallow they really were. God's plumb line would make evident to Israel how far they had deviated from righteousness.

I. An Out-Of-Plumb Society

Have you seen the polls? Time and again we read that America is a very spiritual nation. We even brag about it on our coins: "In

God we trust." We bandy phrases about spirituality and about God on the television talk shows, but one sometimes wonders which god is meant. In America we speak of God when we pledge allegiance, and we speak to God when we get into trouble or when we want to impress the masses. But, how much of it is legitimate? How much has validity? How much has depth? How is it that while the polls show the number of "born-again Christians" increasing, morality in America is at a low ebb? Is it not that we are morally and spiritually a nation adrift? In many ways we reflect eighth century B.C. Israel. We are economically prosperous. We have more money than any nation in history. The worst of our houses luxurious by standards in many other countries. Militarily, we are strong and secure. We live lives of luxury and leisure, but our commitment to God is often casual and half-hearted. How is it they describe us overseas? "In America, Christianity is 3,000 miles wide and a half-inch deep!" We are not at all what we like to think we are. We are out of plumb with God's design for us. The words of another ancient prophet need to be sounded again in America:

> *When the Lord your God has brought you into the land that he swore to your ancestors ... a land with fine, large cities that you did not build, houses filled with all sorts of goods that you did not fill, hewn cisterns that you did not hew, vineyards and olive groves that you did not plant — and when you have eaten your fill, take care that you do not forget the Lord.*
> — Deuteronomy 6:10-12

Even in the church we are leaning out of plumb. Our theology tends to be shallow and our sermons are often designed to be inoffensive. Oh, we don't mind speaking out against issues, so long as we are reasonably certain that what we say will not offend the people of power in our congregations. A friend of mine heard about one preacher who apologized to a prominent person in her congregation by saying, "Well, had I known you might be here today I can assure you I would have never said what I did." It reminded me of those television and movie disclaimers that say, "Any resemblance to persons alive or dead is purely coincidental." Ecclesiastical success often is judged by all the wrong standards, and we strive for warped goals. We worry about temporary prosperity symbols and seek them over that which is eternal. God calls us to repentance, beginning not in the White House but in the church house: "If my people who are called by my name humble themselves, pray, seek my face, and turn from their wicked ways, then I will hear from heaven, and will forgive their sin and heal their land" (2 Chronicles 7:14).

II. What A Difference A Call Makes!

How far different Amos was from the run-of-the-mill preachers of his time! There was a reason why God had to reach down into the hinterlands to raise up a prophet for the capital city. It was simply that the capital city prophets were wimpish and ineffective. Notice, for example, Amaziah, the chief priest of Bethel. Bethel means "God's house."

> *Amaziah, the priest of Bethel, sent to King Jeroboam of Israel, saying, "Amos has conspired against you in the very center of the house of Israel; the land is not able to bear all his words. For thus Amos has said, 'Jeroboam shall die by the sword, and Israel must go into exile away from his land.'"* — Amos 7:10-11

Amaziah had lost all interest in hearing God's word. Already he had sold his soul to King Jeroboam II, one of the cruelest leaders in all history. Jeroboam II held the throne for more than forty years and was credited with the wave of economic and military prosperity Israel enjoyed while he was in power. Amaziah, whose name means "God is strong," had forgotten the message that was in his name. Lacking the intestinal fortitude to speak out against Jeroboam's cruelty and interested only in maintaining his position, he did more than simply stay silent. He became a traitor against God's servant Amos. He twisted what Amos said and reported to the king what was, in fact, a lie. What is it they say? "The first casualty in every war is truth." This was one more example of the truth of that old adage. It is amazing how we can misquote and reform the words of another when we feel a need to save our own positions. Next Amaziah came to confront Amos in the name of the king — although, interestingly enough, Scripture never records an actual meeting between Amaziah and the king. "Amaziah said to Amos, 'O seer, go, flee away to the land of Judah, earn your bread there, and prophesy there; but never again prophesy at Bethel, for it is the king's sanctuary, and it is a temple of the kingdom' " (Amos 7:12-13).

What Amaziah did not count on was that Amos would not back away. Whether or not Amaziah had a commission from his king to run Amos away, we do not know. This we do know: Amos had a commission from the King of kings.

> *"I am no prophet, nor a prophet's son; but I am a herdsman, and a dresser of sycamore trees, and the Lord took me from following the flock, and the Lord said to me, 'Go, prophesy to my people Israel.' Now therefore hear the word of the Lord. You say, 'Do not prophesy against Israel, and do not preach against the house of Isaac.' Therefore thus says the Lord: 'Your wife shall become a prostitute in the city, and your sons and your daughters shall fall by the sword, and your land shall be parceled out by line; you yourself shall die in an unclean land, and Israel shall surely go into exile away from its land.' "* — Amos 7:14-17

This was one major difference between Amaziah and Amos. Amaziah pursued position, while Amos was in a position that pursued him. "I am no prophet, nor a prophet's son; but I am a herdsman, and a dresser of sycamore trees, and the Lord took me from following the flock, and the Lord said to me, 'Go, prophesy to my people Israel.' "

There is another significant difference too: Amaziah pursued his own agenda. He was concerned about his position. Amos pursued God's agenda. "The Lord said to me, 'Go, prophesy to my people Israel.' " The focus of Amos's message was God, not himself.

"We do not proclaim ourselves; we proclaim Jesus Christ as Lord and ourselves as your slaves for Jesus' sake" (2 Corinthians

4:5). Paul was telling the Corinthians that the focus of preaching is Christ, not himself. When you talk about religion, tell people who Christ is and what he did more than you tell about your own accomplishments. He was God. He came to earth because God loved us. He died on the cross for us. He rose again and conquered death. Take on the mindset of another great man of God, John the Baptist: "He must increase, but I must decrease" (John 3:30). Make God's Son, Jesus, your focus.

Amos was not a preacher but a layman. It's amazing to see how many times in Scripture and in the history of the church that God bypasses the clergy and raises up a layperson when he has a really important task to do. What images flood your mind when you hear the term, "a great Christian"? Do you immediately think of a famous evangelist, a missionary, a well-known theologian or some "professional" Christian? Amos the herdsman stands in the company of David the shepherd lad, Rahab the harlot, Nehemiah the wine steward, Charles Finney the lawyer, Dwight L. Moody the shoe salesclerk, and thousands of other people the world calls "ordinary." With God there are no "ordinary" people. Each one is special and each has a call. Perhaps today God is calling you to step out and become his servant in some wonderful way that will accomplish great things for him? Have you let God know that you are available? If not, why not do it now?

When God wants to fill someone and skill someone and thrill someone;
When God wants to mold someone to play the noblest part;
When God longs with all his heart
To create so brave and bold a one that all the world will be amazed;
Watch his methods! Watch his ways!

He persistently perfects whom he royally elects;
How he bends but never breaks,
And God's goodness undertakes.
How God uses whom he chooses;
And with every crisis, he induces

> *And with each blessing he infuses, to try his splendor out.*
> *Oh! God knows what he's about!* — Unknown

We've all met people like Amaziah, those outwardly religious types who sell their souls to climb the ladders of power, prestige, and pride. Often such people wear the external robes of righteousness that make them look like true followers of Jesus. They learn the language of faith and bandy it about to suit their self-centered purposes. Yet, they do not have a deep and lasting relationship with God through his Son, Jesus. There are Amaziahs in every church. They relish positions of visibility and leadership, but they do not know the One who is the King and Head of the church and who went to the cross to redeem it for himself. Perhaps God leaves them among us to remind us how even the mighty are susceptible to falling when they fail to measure themselves daily against God's plumb line. And we have all known people like Amos, dedicated servants of God called with a holy passion and an urgency to do his work and speak the truth for God, who has a plumb line for us. For them, Paul's words hold true: "If I proclaim the gospel, this gives me no ground for boasting, for an obligation is laid on me, and woe to me if I do not proclaim the gospel! For if I do this of my own will, I have a reward; but if not of my own will, I am entrusted with a commission" (1 Corinthians 9:16-17).

III. God's Ever-present Plumb Line

Today God still has a plumb line. His plumb line for us is Jesus, the only unfailingly true and perfect One who ever lived.

> *He is the image of the invisible God, the firstborn of all creation; for in him all things in heaven and on earth were created, things visible and invisible, whether thrones or dominions or rulers or powers — all things have been created through him and for him. He himself is before all things, and in him all things hold together. He is the head of the body, the church; he is the beginning, the firstborn from the dead, so that he might come*

to have first place in everything. For in him all the fullness of God was pleased to dwell, and through him God was pleased to reconcile to himself all things, whether on earth or in heaven, by making peace through the blood of his cross. — Colossians 1:15-20

Jesus knows well the depth to which we are willing to go with God and the straightness of our walk with him. He is the Cornerstone of the church and the Master Architect of the universe. It is he who builds character within us and he alone who made the sacrifice that was necessary to straighten us out when we were crooked and out of sync with God.

Is your life leaning in the wrong direction? Come to the great plumb line, Jesus. Put your life in his hands. Give him your struggles and find new strength to live on the straight and narrow path that leads to eternal life in his presence forevermore.

Lectionary Preaching After Pentecost

The following index will aid the user of this book in matching the correct Sunday with the appropriate text during Pentecost. All texts in this book are from the series for the First Reading, Revised Common Lectionary. (Note that the ELCA division of Lutheranism is now following the Revised Common Lectionary.) The Lutheran designations indicate days comparable to Sundays on which Revised Common Lectionary Propers or Ordinary Time designations are used.

(Fixed dates do not pertain to Lutheran Lectionary)

Fixed Date Lectionaries *Revised Common (including ELCA)* *and Roman Catholic*	Lutheran Lectionary *Lutheran*
The Day of Pentecost	The Day of Pentecost
The Holy Trinity	The Holy Trinity
May 29-June 4 — Proper 4, Ordinary Time 9	Pentecost 2
June 5-11 — Proper 5, Ordinary Time 10	Pentecost 3
June 12-18 — Proper 6, Ordinary Time 11	Pentecost 4
June 19-25 — Proper 7, Ordinary Time 12	Pentecost 5
June 26-July 2 — Proper 8, Ordinary Time 13	Pentecost 6
July 3-9 — Proper 9, Ordinary Time 14	Pentecost 7
July 10-16 — Proper 10, Ordinary Time 15	Pentecost 8
July 17-23 — Proper 11, Ordinary Time 16	Pentecost 9
July 24-30 — Proper 12, Ordinary Time 17	Pentecost 10
July 31-Aug. 6 — Proper 13, Ordinary Time 18	Pentecost 11
Aug. 7-13 — Proper 14, Ordinary Time 19	Pentecost 12
Aug. 14-20 — Proper 15, Ordinary Time 20	Pentecost 13
Aug. 21-27 — Proper 16, Ordinary Time 21	Pentecost 14
Aug. 28-Sept. 3 — Proper 17, Ordinary Time 22	Pentecost 15
Sept. 4-10 — Proper 18, Ordinary Time 23	Pentecost 16
Sept. 11-17 — Proper 19, Ordinary Time 24	Pentecost 17
Sept. 18-24 — Proper 20, Ordinary Time 25	Pentecost 18

Sept. 25-Oct. 1 — Proper 21, Ordinary Time 26	Pentecost 19
Oct. 2-8 — Proper 22, Ordinary Time 27	Pentecost 20
Oct. 9-15 — Proper 23, Ordinary Time 28	Pentecost 21
Oct. 16-22 — Proper 24, Ordinary Time 29	Pentecost 22
Oct. 23-29 — Proper 25, Ordinary Time 30	Pentecost 23
Oct. 30-Nov. 5 — Proper 26, Ordinary Time 31	Pentecost 24
Nov. 6-12 — Proper 27, Ordinary Time 32	Pentecost 25
Nov. 13-19 — Proper 28, Ordinary Time 33	Pentecost 26
	Pentecost 27
Nov. 20-26 — Christ the King	Christ the King

Reformation Day (or last Sunday in October) is October 31 (Revised Common, Lutheran)

All Saints' Day (or first Sunday in November) is November 1 (Revised Common, Lutheran, Roman Catholic)

Books In This Cycle C Series

GOSPEL SET

Praying For A Whole New World
Sermons For Advent/Christmas/Epiphany
William G. Carter

Living Vertically
Sermons For Lent/Easter
John N. Brittain

Changing A Paradigm — Or Two
Sermons For Sundays After Pentecost (First Third)
Glenn E. Ludwig

Topsy-Turvy: Living In The Biblical World
Sermons For Sundays After Pentecost (Middle Third)
Thomas A. Renquist

Ten Hits, One Run, Nine Errors
Sermons For Sundays After Pentecost (Last Third)
John E. Berger

FIRST LESSON SET

The Presence In The Promise
Sermons For Advent/Christmas/Epiphany
Harry N. Huxhold

Deformed, Disfigured, And Despised
Sermons For Lent/Easter
Carlyle Fielding Stewart III

Two Kings And Three Prophets For Less Than A Quarter
Sermons For Sundays After Pentecost (First Third)
Robert Leslie Holmes

What If What They Say Is True?
Sermons For Sundays After Pentecost (Middle Third)
John W. Wurster

A Word That Sets Free
Sermons For Sundays After Pentecost (Last Third)
Mark Ellingsen

SECOND LESSON SET
You Have Mail From God!
Sermons For Advent/Christmas/Epiphany
Harold C. Warlick, Jr.

Hope For The Weary Heart
Sermons For Lent/Easter
Henry F. Woodruff

A Hope That Does Not Disappoint
Sermons For Sundays After Pentecost (First Third)
Billy D. Strayhorn

Big Lessons From Little-Known Letters
Sermons For Sundays After Pentecost (Middle Third)
Kirk W. Webster

Don't Forget This!
Robert R. Kopp
Sermons For Sundays After Pentecost (Last Third)

www.ingramcontent.com/pod-product-compliance
Lightning Source LLC
Chambersburg PA
CBHW071742040426
42446CB00012B/2441